The Iron house – Jane Canna Melbourne

Cresy Cannan

Born Jane Claude in Liverpool, she grew up in **Ambleside**, her family close friends of eccentric intellectuals such as Harriet Martineau and Hartley Coleridge.

Jane's letters and drawings, collected in the National Library of Australia and Oxford University tell her story in this book. It is also the story of the Huguenot Claude family, and its mercantile network that stretched via Liverpool from Gdansk and Berlin to Valparaiso in Chile.

Jane's husband was an agent in the iron buildings trade; together they sailed to Australia during the chaos of the goldrush, Melbourne had become 'totally unfit for genteel people' and Jane had to adapt to 'colonial' life in her own corrugated iron cottage.

Bugloss Publishing, 2013, now £5.99
185 pages, paperback.25 illustrations.
ISBN 978-0-9574046-0-1

To order: www.buglossbooks.com
To contact the author info@buglossbooks.com or 01297 24061

The Iron house – Jane Cannan and the rush to Melbourne

Craig Cannan

Born Jane Claude in Liverpool, she grew up in Ambleside, her family close friends of eccentric intellectuals such as Harriet Martineau and Hartley Coleridge.

Jane's letters and drawings, collected in the National Library of Australia and Oxford University tell her story in this book. It is also the story of the Huguenot Claude family, and its mercantile network that stretched via Liverpool from Gdansk and Berlin to Valparaiso in Chile.

Jane's husband was an agent in the iron buildings trade; together they sailed to Australia during the chaos of the goldrush. Melbourne had become 'totally unfit for genteel people' and Jane had to adapt to colonial life in her own corrugated iron cottage.

Bugloss Publishing, 2013, now £5.99
185 pages, paperback, 25 illustrations
ISBN 978-0-9574046-0-1

To order: www.buglossbooks.com
To contact the author info@buglossbooks.com or 0? 20? 2?00?

The Iron House

The Iron House

Jane Cannan
and the rush to Melbourne

CRESCY CANNAN

Bugloss Publishing, Devon,
with Bloomings Books, Melbourne

Acknowledgements

The following institutions have kindly given permission for my use of materials in their possession:

Bristol Reference Library (Clift-House Iron Works/Braikenridge Collection).
Friends' Historical Library, Dublin (Alfred Webb Autobiography and papers).
Harry Ransom Humanities Research Center, University of Texas at Austin (Hartley Coleridge Collection).
London School of Economics (Harriet Martineau papers).
National Library of Australia, Canberra (David and Jane Cannan letters MS 401; Jane Cannan Pictures LOC 8640, 4564/555-1, 558, 567, 736, 764, 772, 778; Andrew Pollock 'Observations' 642508).
Newnham College, University of Cambridge (A.J. Clough papers).
Royal Historical Society of Victoria (Jane Cannan picture collection).
Sauk County Historical Society, Wisconsin (Louis J. Claude journals).
The President and Fellows of Trinity College, University of Oxford (Cannan Archive, DD262).
University College, University of London (Edwin Chadwick collection).

Those people named below have helped in many and valuable ways, from reading and commenting on drafts, to copying and sharing pictures and papers; from translating German to deciphering archaic script; from linking up knowledge of ancestors to sharing material from their own research, and with technical and design advice. Their expertise, generosity and encouragement to continue with the project have been crucial to its eventually seeing the light of day:

Fergus Cannan
Nick Cannan
Rosel Cannan
James Catmur
Hugh England
Diana Farr
Walburg Fielden
Warwick Forge
Clare Hopkins
Julia Johnson
Michael Leonard
Miles Lewis
Nigel Nixon
Amanda Parrish
Sue Ross
Judith Smart
Gill Sutherland
Jane Tatam
Barbara Todd
Christopher Wells
Eleanor Wells
Carole Woods
Eleanor Wright

Contents

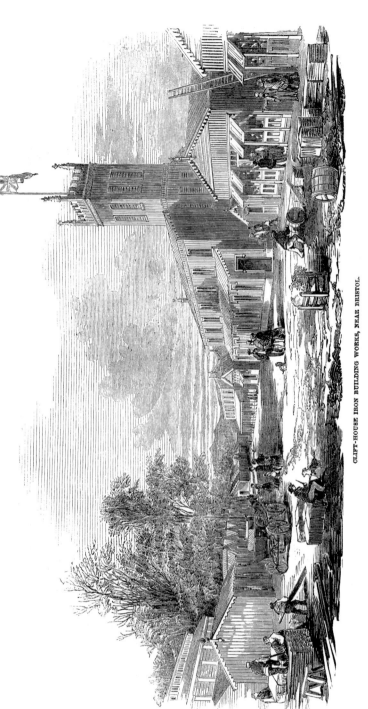

CLIFT-HOUSE IRON BUILDING WORKS, NEAR BRISTOL.

1 Clift-House iron buildings manufactory, Bristol. 'It is difficult to describe the impression produced by the busy scene: a town rising and falling in a week.' Crowds admired Hemming's portable churches, merchants' premises, parsonage, cottages, villas, hotels, and a female emigrants' home, all ready to be speedily disassembled and packed for shipment to Melbourne. (Illustrated London News, 18 February 1854)

Foreword

To picture the British pioneers of the Australian colonies as stuffy Victorians is a serious mistake. They were overwhelmingly young and enterprising. They varied in social status from the remittance men despatched by embarrassed noble families, through the younger sons of farming families, and urban clerks, down to sturdy artisans, often with Chartist leanings. But their almost universal characteristics were enterprise, and a sense of adventure.

Jane Cannan, the heroine of this story, wrote 'I have such an affection for the little ugly iron house that I am half afraid to leave it.' Her contemporaries in Melbourne included Sarah Bunbury, living in a farmhouse outside Melbourne with furniture patched up from trunks, and trying to grow enough produce to feed the family and the maidservant. On the goldfields were women diggers who dressed as men to escape attention. Their male equivalents included enterprising squatters from middle class backgrounds, who positively revelled in travelling through the bush unshaven, and resembling bushrangers more than gentlemen.

Despite the greater fluidity of society, the unusual economic conditions of the 1850s, and the more benign climate, both Adelaide and Melbourne were very British cities. The language, the laws, the social conventions and the food were all more or less British. While British visitors sometimes discerned a degree of Americanisation in Melbourne, American visitors never doubted that it was British. Even a hundred years later Australians who had never left the country would speak of a visit to England as 'going home'. In the nineteenth century English companies, like Doultons, the potters, would send a family member or senior staffer to manage the Melbourne branch, just like the Manchester one, though the person in question might be a little younger. David Cannan, a relative by marriage of one of his firm's partners, is an example of this practice.

The personal story of the Cannans is interesting in itself. I first came across Jane's sketches when I was asked to advise on a collection of them which had been rediscovered in the holdings of the Royal Historical Society of Victoria, and I then made a point of reviewing the other material held at the Australian National Library. She had drawn local scenes such as the Richmond Bridge, and Gertrude Street, Collingwood (now Fitzroy), and also a number of prominent houses in Melbourne, such as Bishopscourt, and Toorak House, soon to be the official residence of Governor Hotham. Some of these are the best, or even the only record of buildings which were quite prominent in their time.

Jane Cannan had also made a point of drawing examples of the Morewood & Rogers products, including a number of buildings roofed in their tiles, others such as the Collegiate Institution, Adelaide, which were roofed in their corrugated iron, and also complete corrugated iron buildings like the Scots Church, Prahran, and the Cannans' own 'little ugly iron house'. But the two concluding illustrations in the National Library collection, showing the grave of their infant daughter Louisa, tug at the heartstrings. This is a family story as well as one about colonial society, trade and technical innovation.

★

Galvanised iron, so-called, is iron coated in zinc to protect it, but as the result of a protracted patent dispute a decade earlier, the firm of Morewood & Rogers produced a version coated first in tin and then in zinc, 'galvanised tinned iron'. This is the galvanised iron which first reached the Australian colonies in 1851, not in the form of corrugated iron, which was to follow shortly, but as large roofing tiles, with rolls at the edges to seal one over the next. This was the product which David Cannan was first promoting in Adelaide and Melbourne, and after 160 years some of these tiles are still to be seen on roofs.

Morewood & Rogers were entrepreneurs who acquired patents for processes such as stamping and curving corrugated sheets, and had the machines, and the products themselves, manufactured for them by others. After their tiles they exported corrugated iron, and then complete iron buildings to Australia, and especially to Melbourne. They were prefabricators on a small scale compared with others like Samuel Hemming, J.H. Porter, John Walker, and later Francis Morton. But they were part of a remarkable activity. More prefabricated buildings reached Melbourne than had previously been sent to any location in the world. The number sent to California three or four years earlier was much smaller, and all of them have been destroyed, mainly in the devastating San Francisco fires.

In Britain itself there are significant numbers of 'temporary' iron churches and chapels, iron barns and farm buildings – which have been barely documented – and some other structures such as tennis pavilions. But they are from later in the century, barely qualify as prefabricated, and are of very little technical interest. Fortuitously more buildings of the mid-nineteenth century, the great age of prefabrication, survive in Melbourne, and south-eastern Australia generally, than anywhere else in the world. One or two of these are Morewood & Rogers buildings brought out in the time of David and Jane Cannan.

Miles Lewis, AM, FAHA
Emeritus Professor, University of Melbourne
http://www.mileslewis.net/

Illustrations and credits

Introduction

Early in 1853, Jane Dorothea Claude (pronounced 'Clode', in the French manner) sits solemnly for the photographer. Her dark hair is parted severely in the middle and drawn back unflatteringly, Jane having little patience with friends' attempts to soften her face with curls. She already has grey streaks and, with her somewhat heavy features, looks older than her thirty years. For the smart studio in London's Regent Street she wears a rich silk dress with lace collar and cuffs. Her left hand holds a draped shawl – probably, though it is hard to see, displaying her new wedding ring. With her right hand she clutches a

2 Jane Dorothea Cannan, née Claude. A photograph or daguerreotype print with painted embellishments, taken around the time of her marriage. Jane disliked 'finery' and looks uncomfortable in the London studio. She was preoccupied by the enormity of the preparations for the imminent journey to Melbourne. (James Catmur)

capacious handbag, perhaps containing her pencils and sketchbook, notepaper for long and breathless letters, and a 'condition of England' novel to read on her many railway journeys.

This is not Jane's true self but a picture for relatives to remember her by. To the real Jane 'the very idea of being taken & made tidy would drive me out into some wilderness'. She is leaning forward a little, eager to move on from the wearing obligations of the Victorian spinster daughter. Hitherto disappointed, she wants to love and be loved, and to draw rather than wasting her time on 'fancy work'. 'To save my life', she wrote, 'I could not make antimacassars or mats'.[1]

★

When David Alexander Cannan was commissioned by the English firm Morewood & Rogers to sell iron buildings in Australia, Jane jumped at the chance to go with him as his wife. Coming as she did from a mercantile world, her horizons stretched further than Liverpool and Ambleside in northern England's beautiful Lake District where she had hitherto lived. She was prepared to take the risk of marrying an alarmingly thin and financially insecure Scottish accounts clerk. It made sense. The 'surplus women' issue was much discussed at the time amid anxiety that increasing numbers of middle-class women (for lack of eligible husbands or suitable employment in already crowded crafts and professions) were facing dreary lives of financial dependence on fathers, brothers and charities.

Jane's choices were limited, and her own money was modest, but she wanted to travel. When an exhausted Harriet Martineau came home to Ambleside after a fact-finding trip for one of her topical and campaigning articles for her huge readership, she wrote to Jane that she often thought 'with yearning of your offer of terms of partnership – that you shall do all the travelling, & I the writing at home'.[2]

Jane was fully aware of the shocking consequences of Britain's rapid industrialisation, and was involved in charitable visiting, in a housing scheme and in school teaching, being especially fond of and interested in children. In eccentric, literary Ambleside and in Liverpool, among philanthropic mercantile circles, Jane had good connections. The poet

3 David Alexander Cannan. A daguerreotype taken in 1853. A Scot from lowland Galloway, pale David's health was never strong. We can discern in his steady gaze a rather defiant nature and impatience with 'humbug'; his talent in mathematics led to employment as an accounts clerk in Manchester. (James Catmur)

Hartley Coleridge, an intimate family friend, observed that, despite her diligence, Jane was not 'the regular philanthropic Miss [...] She never interferes with the Parson's business.'[3] She had a wit envied by her friend and fellow teacher Annie Clough (a pioneer of women's university education at Cambridge), which leavened any earnestness, though she shared Annie's sense of the necessity to get on with 'the much that might be done'.[4] A sense of her own apartness, of being an outsider, however, infuses her writing – but it is that characteristic which enabled her to leave us her acute observations of a rapidly changing world.

★

My research started when my aunt gave me copies of Jane's drawings which are held at Australia's Royal Historical Society of Victoria. They included one of the corrugated iron house in which Jane and David had lived in Melbourne from 1854-7.

I have always had a fondness for cottages, whether in the English vernacular of local brick or stone or cob or meandering timber, roofed in soft thatch or clay tiles, or the tiny wooden weather-boarded shacks of rural Tasmania. As a child in post-war London I noticed neat little 'prefabs' erected in bombed-out areas; these cleverly designed working-class homes with generous gardens stood out as neighbourly and green sites in what then seemed a grimy, impersonal city.

What I rarely saw in England were corrugated iron houses. Farm buildings yes, corrugated iron roofing over collapsing thatch, rusting 'tin tabernacles', damp mission halls, musty sports pavilions and wonky allotment shacks. So how did my ancestor – whose family had a rather large stone house in Ambleside – come to live in the stark little iron house in Australia, a version of which is preserved by the National Trust in Melbourne?[5] How did she feel about its utilitarian design, about its industrial materials and construction method, when she had hitherto enjoyed drawing the 'natural', organic disorder of the (usually damp) rustic cottages eulogised by the romantic, simple lifers? Was there, in fact, a degree of, as Herbert puts it, naïve appeal, an honesty and directness, which earned these little cottages, some gently ornamented, affection from their inhabitants and a recognition that they were 'not entirely innocent of architectural merit'?[6]

Intrigued, I discovered that more drawings were in the National Library of Australia in Canberra, together with letters, and that a further stash of letters was in Trinity College, Oxford University. Thanks to the internet and digitised newspapers, I was able to add background to the story, and to trace papers of contemporaries such

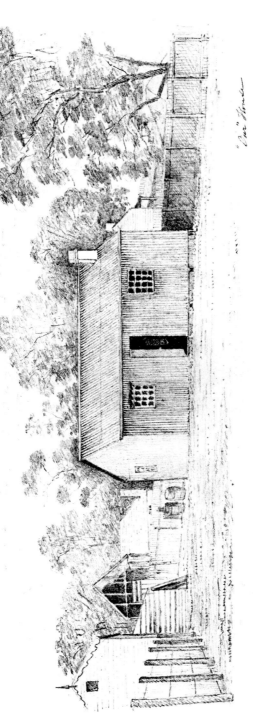

"Our" house

4 Jane Cannan: "*Our*" *house'. Assembled in late 1853 on a spacious suburban plot in south east Melbourne's Prahran, this house was rented from David Cannan's employer, Morewood & Rogers. These little portable, galvanised corrugated iron-clad cottages, exported in their thousands, met an urgent housing need among civil servants and those in commerce. (Royal Historical Society of Victoria)* as David Cannan's colleague Andrew Pollock. Distant Cannan relatives shared the daguerreotypes, drawings and assorted portraits that have been passed down their lines.

So we know what Jane and David looked like, despite the formal poses. And we know that they were not 'worldly-minded' and were dismissive of empty display or vacuous conversation. They preferred a good book to parties, and their aim in life was to live in a modest house of their own in the countryside.

Slowly transcribing the material in these collections enabled me to let Jane tell the story of her wider family in Prussia and Chile, of her youth in Liverpool and the Lake District, and of her life in Melbourne. The cramped, scrawled, sometimes crossed and faded script was often declaredly dashed off because another letter was owed to a friend or a relative needed attention, or a train had to be caught with perhaps a child to escort.

Although not a journal, Jane's letters have something of that quality, many being accounts to be passed around the family. Others are more private and reflective, giving some edge to the encouraging picture that emigrants so often felt obliged to send home.[7] David Cannan represents a particular segment of the hundreds of thousands who migrated during the period: not the poverty-stricken people intending to settle, but rather the insecure middle-class hoping to benefit from new trade with the colonies and to return home with gentlemanly status assured. Jane and her husband tell us about their particular business – the selling of prefabricated iron buildings and associated galvanised iron components; materials which have of course become part of the distinctive Australian heritage.[8]

Jane took her drawing seriously; confident of her skill, she was regularly asked for sketches of views and houses as mementoes. Her eye in Melbourne became atuned to the architectural rather than picturesque aspects of buildings, partly because she was keen to record Morewood & Rogers' buildings *in situ* for the firm. And perhaps she shared something of her brother Louis Claude's engineering talent, which he was using in surveying for new American railroads.

Jane left what is now recognised as a significant record of the

Melbourne area's rapid growth around the time of the gold-rush.[9] Women's amateur sketchbooks, like Jane's, are typically to be found in libraries rather than art galleries.[10] While perhaps not 'Art', Jane's careful sketches have enabled Melbourne historians to trace the stories of the buildings and townscapes that she drew, placing them in the context of Melbourne's subsequent development.[11]

Jane's houses, whether of wood or iron, large or small, capture an era of relatively modest and egalitarian colonial life. Her drawings and her descriptions of daily life illustrate Melbourne's novel low-density suburbia – a world away from sensational newspaper images of wine, women and song of the gold-rush, or of the sturdy, thrifty pioneer in the bush.

★

Jeannette Claude is the younger cousin to whom many of Jane's letters are addressed; they became close during Jeannette's arrival in England in 1849 after nine years in Valparaiso in Chile where the Claudes were wealthy mineral exporters. Jane's other correspondent was her close friend, and David's sister, Mary Cannan, four years her senior. They probably met while Mary was governess to the sons of William Rathbone Greg (of the giant Greg cotton firm) in the Lake District. Through the Claudes, Mary realised her ambition to travel, spending four years in Berlin and Rome, supporting herself by teaching, translating and writing on art and archaeology.[12] Mary can be considered the midwife of this book in that she brought together her brother David and Jane.

Notes on spelling and money

I have spelled Jeannette's name thus, French style, despite Jane and others sometimes rendering it Jeanette or Janetta. Jane is also inconsistent with the spelling of her sister Louise's name: the German form, as in her mother's name, has the same pronunciation as 'Louisa'. Once we throw in Spanish spellings from Chile things get even more complex, hence my decision on consistency. I have left most spelling, punctuation and capitalisation in letters as in the originals except where a change is needed for clarity.

British money was divided into pounds, composed of twenty shillings (rendered /-), with twelve pence (expressed as 'd') to the shilling.

ONE

A Huguenot childhood: Liverpool

In August 1853, after three months under sail, Jane Cannan at last smelled land. Birds and insects began to appear. Their ship converged with smaller local vessels, and with *Mercia* and *Caroline Glen* also out from Britain. Suddenly the Australian coast was in sight and then a lighthouse. Passengers began to pack. The cabin – the Cannans' first home of their own and which, despite the storms and rough conditions, Jane would remember with fondness – was now miserably bare. Her worn-out blue silk and red merino dresses were rescued from being thrown into the sea by needier passengers.

The pilot came on board and was pressed for news of the colony of Victoria by passengers who had made a huge leap of faith in undertaking this journey. Was it worrying that twenty vessels had arrived the previous day, and six or seven the same day as *Hempsyke*? And that these vessels had brought migrants not just from Britain and Ireland but from America and China? For David this was excellent news: there would be huge demand for Morewood & Rogers' houses. The pilot assured him that in Melbourne 'anything from a tent to a Galvanized Iron house [is] selling at great profits'.[13]

After a final dinner on board, the Cannans wrote David's mother a letter to be despatched next day, whatever the cost, to announce their safe arrival. Jane reflected that:

5 Louis Claude, 1792-1828. Jane's father was born in Berlin into a Huguenot mercantile family. He moved to the great port of Liverpool as a commission agent. He died in Marseille, France, leaving five young children. (Eleanor Wright)

6 Jane's mother Louise Auguste Claude, née Pfeffer, 1800-1873. Mrs Claude's father was a Berlin sculptor; there she married before moving to Liverpool. Widowed at the age of twenty-eight, she lived all her subsequent life in England's Lake District, in Ambleside, supported by her brother-in-law's Chilean mining business. (James Catmur)

We have got through the voyage splendidly and I am sure I must be well prepared for commencing housekeeping after my experience here where my domains were so seldom passive under my rule. It must be easier to manage three houses than one cabin…The first impression of Australia is much more agreeable than I expected…I was delighted to see wooded hills, one range behind another, and glens opening up into them, like any Scotch coast, it was a showery day too and the clouds lying low on the hills made it look more home like.[14]

Along with many emigrants, Jane and David found it reassuring to liken the first glimpse of the new land to 'home'.[15] Jane's comparison was perhaps intended to reassure her mother-in-law that she shared David's nostalgia for his native Scotland. Writing, however, at the same time to her cousin Jeannette, she mentioned an area of the English coastline which was more familiar to her.

'Home', though, was not a straightforward concept in Jane's scattered family.

★

Jane's father Louis Claude, portrayed as a handsome, dandyish young man with curly hair, book in hand, was descended from a family of Huguenots with their roots in Metz in eastern France. During the French persecutions of Protestants in the 1680s Prussia encouraged Huguenot immigration, the city of Berlin subsequently prospering through this skilled, educated and intermarried minority whose faith centred on the teachings of Calvin.

Jane's mother Louise Auguste Pfeffer was a pretty, fine-featured young woman. A second cousin of Louis Claude, she had been baptised in the Huguenot French Church in Berlin where the couple married. Their first child, Anne, was born in Liverpool in 1819, their second, Mary Sophia, in Prussia, and the next three – Jane (in 1822), Louise and Louis James – in Liverpool.

Louis Claude and his brothers Adolphe and Charles were merchants who moved between Liverpool, Danzig and Berlin, taking advantage of the upsurge in these ports' trade during the Napoleonic wars.[16] Liverpool directories list Louis Claude's premises in the Salthouse Dock.[17] His will named William Rathbone as a valued friend, so presumably he was involved in commodity trading with or for the great Rathbone enterprise.

Observers such as de Tocqueville marvelled at Liverpool's enormous, crowded waterfront and the huge variety of goods that were handled. Visitors could wander through the great dock system and watch cargoes from around the world being unloaded; comparisons with Venice prompted the response that Liverpool's great forests of masts and spars embodied far more impressive activity.[18] As the port expanded the grand 'old' merchant dynasties moved away from their counting houses and homes around the docks. That area's crowded courts and cellars were increasingly occupied by emigrants awaiting a ship, with rising desperation during the economic slump of the 'hungry forties' and the Irish potato famine. Liverpool's merchant society now centred on particular chapels and churches, notably the non-conformist Unitarians of Renshaw Street, closely associated with the Rathbone and Holt dynasties.[19] Education, including of girls, business acumen, science, writing and social reform were strong features of Unitarianism, a culture close to that of the Huguenots. Such was the world of the Claude family, who lived during Jane's early childhood at Park Hill Road in Toxteth Park, then an area of comfortable merchants' houses.

The trade directories cite no particular commodities for Louis Claude – and perhaps there was no specialism, given that at the time the Rathbones were, in addition to cotton importing, trading in turpentine, tar, ashes, apples, flour and flaxseed from the USA, in hides from Montevideo, in wheat from Ireland, the Baltic and Canada, in oats and barley from Ireland, in mahogany from Belize, and in sugar from Demerara. Louis' brother Charles was associated with the Liverpool merchant Charles Tayleur, a significant importer of cotton from the USA, and of wool and hides from South America.[20] They were beginning to establish the partnership Tayleur, Claude y

Compañia in Chile, a firm which soon became a major exporter of gold and silver and was to be a lifeline for the Claude family.[21]

Jane's father and his business partner Edward Pearson were among many business casualties in those turbulent economic times, and were declared insolvent in 1822.[22] Nevertheless, Mrs Claude's picture of her family of four little daughters is one of affectionate gaiety. Reporting the birth, finally, of a son just before Christmas 1825 to a relative in Germany, she described the happy disorder in their 'madhouse':

> The racket is hard to bear, especially when the parrot and the turtledoves join the chorus of the children…That all of us are very pleased with <u>our</u> Christ child you well know – Louis was beside himself – even I could hardly recover from that joyful fright…Today the boy is six weeks old and is beginning to look like a child, especially beautiful he isn't yet, but he is coming to resemble Papa, I think…He will be baptised and will be given the names Louis James. It will be a splendid confusion with the four Lu's in the house…
>
> Naturally, I could not be with the children at the scene for Christmas Eve, but even so, their joy was so noisy, I could hear them upstairs. Afterwards, they came upstairs with their dolls and Louise was especially happy.[23]

Better fortune came Louis Claude's way for his will refers to an estate of some £3,000. But disaster followed – in January 1828, when Jane was five, he died in Marseille in France, probably while working for the Rathbones. The widowed Mrs Claude, only twenty eight and with five young children, was now acutely aware that she was dependent on the goodwill of her brother-in-law Charles Claude and of her children's guardian, the Liverpool sugar-king James Brancker.

★

Ambleside in the Lake District was the kind of place where genteel 'economy' was socially acceptable. While it concealed fabulously rich merchants and industrialists from Manchester and Liverpool in mansions around the beautiful lake Windermere, it also had its high-minded literary set – the Wordsworths in particular, and the Arnolds of Rugby School fame. The Claudes moved into Rothay Bank, when Jane was six, and she was always to remember the wonderful freedom of roaming over the magnificent fells.

In a period when German poetry and philosophy were transforming western world-views, the ability to read and translate German was a considerable social asset. Hartley Coleridge, the 'marvellously odd', strikingly imaginative poet, son of his more famous father Samuel Taylor Coleridge, wrote to his mother that Mrs Claude, his 'dear lady', was 'a most kind friend of mine, with whom I am studying German.'[24] The Claudes counted among the households – another being the lakeside faux-gothic mansion of his patron James Brancker – where Hartley Coleridge could drop in and settle down in a chair, accepted and loved, drunk or sober. The Claudes' stock of books and journals nourished him. He loved babies, young girls and family gossip, and this domesticity of widowed mother and 'four sweet daughters and a noble John Bull of a boy' – balanced his hermit nature.[25] His letters contain curious observations such as a little girl having 'learned to knit in the Prussian fashion introduced by Mrs Claude.'[26]

Mrs Claude responded to his friendship with long and detailed letters about her children's health, development and education. Thus we learn something of Jane's childhood, although less is said of her than of her nervy, literary older sister Mary, of her wild younger sister Louise, and of Louis James, the son and hope of the family. Perhaps sensible Jane, the middle child, was left to fend for herself but, nevertheless, her mother enjoyed her ability to 'scrape the boards clean upon the subject in hand.'[27] When she was sixteen Hartley Coleridge asked Mrs Claude 'Does Jane prosper in her drawing, and is she as witty as ever?'[28] Jane later recollected that a governess had described her as 'fond of her own way'. She knew that she was an insular person who found it difficult to express affection, and thought that it might have been 'owing to not having been caressed in infancy'.[29] Her young widowed mother would have been preoccupied with the younger children, and it was her older sister Annie who particularly cared for Jane.

This sister's harrowing illness and death in the York Asylum was a dreadful blow to the family when Jane was seventeen. As a young woman, when she saw happy couples she found tears in her eyes, feeling she was not destined for love, 'and when I get to my bedside I say to one with whom nothing is abstract Lay thy hand on my head and bless me for none of my fellow creatures will'.[30]

Mrs Claude took her family back to Liverpool, to Falkner Street 36 as she put it in the German style. Mary complained bitterly to Hartley Coleridge that while her brother Louis was fond of school, she was not at all reconciled to living in the city, that they had discovered no pretty walks, and while they had been to an exhibition, the pictures were generally frightful. There was, however, some compensation in a piano and musical neighbours, and in going with Mr Brancker to see the great new steamers and 'the American Packets which are so beautifully fitted up it quite makes one long to go on a voyage.' And their younger cousins, Adolphe Claude's children (Jeannette, Dick, Adolphe, Charles and Willy and their mother 'Tante' or Aunt Minne) had arrived in town, on their way from Berlin to Chile. They had forgotten their English and 'are chattering German as fast and funnily as possible.'[31]

With a Huguenot background the Claude family would have valued frugality, hard work, personal responsibility, high quality craftsmanship, and education.[32] While close to the Liverpool Unitarians, Mrs Claude and her family took to attending the Anglican church for reasons we do not know. The Claude girls would have been taught mainly at home, largely by their mother, supplemented by a governess and masters for drawing, music and languages. Mrs Claude told her sister-in-law that Annie went to a German school in the mornings and also learnt geography, English history and arithmetic, the hopes being that she might have gone to the Luisenstift, a prestigious girls' school in Berlin.[33] Jane and her sister Mary became far more interested in books, drawing and serious discussion than the 'fancy-work' and the limited 'accomplishments' which then passed as education for girls.[34]

Mrs Claude was quick to involve herself and her children in the rich cultural life of Liverpool. She took her family to the city's Royal Institution for the Promotion of Literature, Science and the Arts, telling Hartley Coleridge that it was:

> patronised by all classes…the rooms were lighted up with gas very handsomely – pictures, prints – curiosities of art & nature were furnished by the individuals interested in it to fill up all the empty spaces & a lecture was advertised for a certain evening after which tea & coffee would be served… The first lecture was upon Geology…but it was so well known to every body & the lecturer a dull & nervous man – it was very uninteresting – but there was a galvanic battery & various other amusements for the curious – amongst which I belonged nor did I rest till I had tried the effects of the said battery and shocked Mary very much by doing so – she thought it would be much better to try it upon some of the dead reptiles in the next room.[35]

Looking forward to 'lectures on vocal harmony – then come "animal mechanics" & then magnetic electricity…There will be some…upon German Literature to which I intend taking Mary who really is a very good German', Mrs Claude commented that these soirées afforded people 'another reason for passing an evening from home – showing their finery & their daughters off & having a topic for conversation next day.'[36]

★

Of her daughters Mary, Jane, and Louise's progress and the amusement they found as a family, Mrs Claude was positive. But her son Louis was another matter. His early education in Ambleside may have been with kindly schoolmaster Mr Dawes who, as Harriet Martineau discovered, was prone to leave notices on the school door marked 'Gone a-fishing' with a suggestion to follow him.[37] In Liverpool Louis attended the Academy which he appeared to enjoy, yet he also, Mrs

Claude remarked, 'has the most extraordinary fancies now & then & his notion of free will is by no means abated since we came here.'[38] For Louis wanted to learn engineering. This was not a gentlemanly pursuit, though all around them in Liverpool the new marvels of the industrial age were evident, and the old merchant families were increasing their empires by investing in ships, railways and bridges.

Miserable letters came to Mrs Claude from a lonely Louis when she sent him to Kings' College School in London.[39] She gave way: at fifteen, Louis was back in Liverpool and an engineering apprentice, probably at the Clarence Foundry of Bury, Curtis and Kennedy, making marine engines. Mr Brancker had bought the necessary tools and Louis, Mrs Claude told Hartley Coleridge, 'is delighted beyond measure just now…a gentleman pattern maker, such is his own expression.'[40] Perhaps Uncle Charles had also helped – he had connections through Tayleur's partnership with George and Robert Stephenson whose Vulcan Foundry was building cutting-edge steam locomotives and ships. Knowing of his uncles' and cousins' journeys by sailing ship to and from Chile, Louis was well aware of the technological revolution that he was participating in.

★

Through her teens, Jane worked on her drawings and watercolours. Her youthful talent shows in a cleverly composed drawing inscribed for her aunt Louise Henri in which the eye is led down a dark path into a churchyard, the church's tower sheltering a dilapidated thatched cottage (see picture number 12). If somewhat derivative of the romantic style then in vogue, Jane's drawings nevertheless already capably depict the structure and setting of buildings.

As well as drawing masters and later lessons from painting parsons such as a Mr Brocklebank, Jane learned from her well-informed and enthusiastic mother whose father, Johann Gottlieb Pfeffer, was a Berlin sculptor. And, furthermore, the Claudes were related by marriage to the Chodowiecki family. In the late eighteenth century, Daniel Chodowiecki had been a highly successful graphic artist and director of the Berlin Academy of Art. Jane was later to remark on her mother's

7 Jane Cannan: 'Near Beddgelert.' Jane's mother took her daughters on several trips to admire romantic Welsh castles and wild scenery during the 1840s. This is near Snowdon, the highest mountain in Wales and England, which Jane drew in the fashionably picturesque style, contrasting dramatic peaks and vernacular cottages. (James Catmur)

acute memory of the great historical scenes they had seen among the paintings in Frankfurt. Mrs Claude envied from the bottom of her soul Jane's friend Mary Cannan wandering among the ruins and statues of Rome, and Jane liked 'to see people chipping marble… sculpture always makes more impression on me than paintings'.[41]

In 1845, Mr Dawes, the Ambleside teacher, died and the Claudes moved into his house, Broadlands. What prompted the move? Was it no longer necessary to be in Liverpool now that Louis had found his feet there? Had Mrs Claude tired of Liverpool's cultural life now that she was middle-aged and complaining of lumbago and rheumatism? Perhaps Jane's younger sister Louise's attachment to the White family was a draw. Captain White was involved with Louis in establishing a paddle steamer company to meet growing demand from tourists (boosted by the construction of the railway) to Windermere and its beautiful lake. McConochie and Claude of Liverpool built *Firefly* and *Dragonfly*, introducing some ill-tempered business rivalry to that genteel resort.[42]

In January 1847, Louise married John White, an assistant surgeon in the Indian Army. The couple sailed with his regiment for Calcutta, Mrs Claude reporting that 'we had the satisfaction of seeing him officiate in his uniform the day of embarkation & he looked wonderfully as if he had never worn anything else but a uniform – no doubt to the great satisfaction of his father!' Louise proved to be a good sailor though other ladies were *hors de combat*. And, to her horror, she had 'the post of honour at the Capt.'s right hand and has to make the move after dinner'.[43]

It was the last time that Jane saw her sister Louise, and the last time that Mrs Claude would see her four surviving children together.

Two

A somewhat Amazonian society: Ambleside and the Lake District

Ambleside was a small but prosperous town in the mid-nineteenth century with a bobbin-making industry, and three inns. Harriet Martineau enthusiastically walked her readers round the little, irregular market square with its ancient cross, pointing out

> the saddler's, the butcher's, the watchmaker's, the linen-draper's, the ironmonger's, and the lawyer's and carrier's offices on the left; and on the right, the coach-office, the baker's, the milliner's, the druggist's and the post-office; which is also the place of books and stationary.

Among the houses of the gentry was Broadlands. The pretty house, with large sash windows designed to admit much-needed light in that often grey region, was, according to a sketch of Jane's, somewhat gloomily obscured by over-enthusiastic ivy and shrubbery. From the grounds were magnificent views over Windermere and the dramatic Loughrigg Fell. Here, Martineau declared, lived hospitable Mrs Claude and her daughters in a place known 'for its care of the sick, and the orphans, and the ignorant.'[44]

Jane's energies however were also absorbed – at the behest of her mother – by her sister's difficulties. Strangely aloof, beautiful, ethereal

Mary disliked travel and strangers, preferring to live quietly, reading German poetry and writing very Victorian natural history stories for children in which suffering featured heavily. [45]

While Mary never married, there may have been *tendresses*. Some years earlier, she had been enraptured by the High Anglican Ambleside clergyman Frederick Faber. [46] Some have speculated that Mary was the object of the poet Arthur Clough's admiration during the summer of 1846 (when he wrote his line 'When panting sighs the bosom fill'). [47] Or did Mary enjoy a romance with worldly Matthew Arnold, once Louis' playmate, now an idling Oxford undergraduate? [48] Arnold family correspondence subsequently mocked Matthew's feelings for Mary, 'the Cruel Invisible'. [49]

Other disturbing episodes seem to feature in Mary's life. Jane referred to the young clergyman Lonsdale Pritt spilling out his rage and indignation to her in a precarious skiff on Windermere, perhaps, she wondered, because he was away from his mission to provide antidotes to the 'vices and ignorance' of Birmingham, or was it to do with his having disturbed Mary Claude 'in that way'? [50] Fortunately Pritt emigrated to New Zealand.

What of Jane during this period? Who occupied her private thoughts? Curiosity is aroused by her reporting some years later that her friend Jane Cooper 'cannot be persuaded out of believing that I have a helpless attachment for Arthur Clough!' [51] Muddled conjecture or some truth in the matter? At later points Jane refers to having 'a history', to having discarded something on a Welsh mountain – an unrequited love perhaps? Jane Cooper was also to report to a third party that she had 'seen Jane in the hardest of trials a young woman could have.' [52] Such were the euphemisms used to refer to broken engagements or jiltings, events that were generally airbrushed out of Victorians' lives.

The Clough family was well-known to the Claudes from Liverpool; both fathers were merchants (Clough in the American cotton-trade), and Jane had formed a close friendship with Arthur's sister Annie. Arthur was both learned and charming. He was a man whose concern over the great issues of the day – child labour, the

Irish famine, crowded and filthy slums, suffrage, and illiteracy – had none of the dismaying austerity of so many in the burgeoning world of Victorian charity. He would have appealed deeply to Jane's interest in 'stirring' people.[53]

The satirical writings of the Scottish essayist Thomas Carlyle were offering answers to a new generation alarmed at the condition of England (a phrase he had coined). Carlyle derided the industrial age's greed and materialism, the 'do-nothing' aristocracy, and the windbag Parliament, and asserted the right to a fair day's wage for a fair day's work. He placed hope in man's freedom to exert his will, to find the answers within himself, challenging traditional church teaching.[54]

Jane's friend Annie Clough did not, like Arthur, shed her Anglican allegiances. However, she began to question the literal reading of the Bible, for instance on eternal punishment and was comforted by Arthur's assurance that 'the Greek words did not mean so much as that.'[55] And Jane, discussing with Martineau her translation of the French philosopher Comte, who was arguing for science as a basis for understanding of human society, found her own faith needed to accommodate science: 'surely the more perfect any of these sciences the more surely we must look for the perfect author – The certainty with which an eclipse may be foretold does not affect the fact that someone made the sun.'[56]

★

At the end of summers, visiting men returned to their larger world of government, universities, industry and travel, and Ambleside resumed its 'Amazonian' aspect. Martineau happily declared, however, that parties were often 'composed wholly of ladies; and they happen to be such ladies as leave nothing to be wished.'[57]

A prolific writer on the great topics of the day, with Huguenot origins and a Unitarian upbringing, Martineau continued to pour out her articles and books. The price of her celebrity was 'unscrupulous strangers' trying to glimpse her by hiding in her shrubbery. She threw herself into a series of lectures aimed at local working people – wheelwrights, saddlers, shoemakers, carpenters, builders, painters

The Knoll
Ambleside
    May day

Dear Mr Cannan

    This will be handed to
you by my young friend,
Alfred Webb, whom I can
confidently recommend to your
good offices. He is an excellent youth,
& clever too. The only faults I
know of in him are faults of
manner, & a too anxious conscientiousness

8 *Probably engraved by Harriet Clarke from a sketch by Hammersley:
This example of Harriet Martineau's enormous correspondence was dashed
off to David Cannan before his voyage to Australia with Jane. Martineau's
notepaper shows her house (The Knoll) and her poultry. A neighbour
of Jane and the Claude family, her Lake District house was in a rugged
landscape much admired by tourists, artists and poets. (Trinity College,
University of Oxford)*

and farmers, with their apprentices and families. Topics included the histories of England and the United States ('with a special view to recommend the Anti-slavery cause'), geography, and sanitary reform.[58] She was an admirer of the tireless public health campaigner and administrator, Edwin Chadwick, whom she knew well from her London days, the 'first of our citizens', she said

> who fairly penetrated the foul region of our sanitary disorders, and set us to work to reform them…He has gone on to supply me with valuable information, from that day to this – from his exposition of the way in which country justices aggravated pauperism under the old [poor] law, to the latest improvement in hollow bricks and diameter of drains.[59]

The fact was that the dark underside to picturesque Ambleside, with its wonderful natural setting and plentiful water, was the dreadful condition of working people's housing. This, and the consequences of men preferring the pub to a squalid home, now engaged Martineau's attention. Rather than charity or poor law assistance, she put 'the people in the way of providing wholesome dwellings for themselves. There was no time to be lost.'[60]

Thus began the Windermere Building Society, a mutual aid scheme into whose running Jane was enlisted, probably for her reliable and quietly diplomatic manner. Jane reported that

> Our beloved president Bell the druggist has got into disgrace with [Miss Martineau] and retired promptly from the Society – He had bought up more of the field than she thought right for his own purposes and as she attacked him rather savagely & he did not quite understand her language – he got vexed and his friends & enemies egged him on till there was a regular little row – Fortunately for me, it was kept out of the public meetings or I should have been awkwardly placed between the druggist who is a particular friend of

mine – and Miss M. who has always been so kind to me…
but Miss M is not quite pleased with me for not going the
whole length with her.[61]

Martineau's other Ambleside scheme was the application of William
Cobbett's concept of cottage economy. She created a small-holding
on a two acre plot, run by a labourer and his wife. She was derided
for the commodious dwelling for the pig which allowed it to exercise
in the sun and to be scrubbed in warm water, and for the pampered
cows, brushed every day until their coats shone. Her scrupulously
clean animals were, to everyone's astonishment, highly productive,
and were immortalised in her successful books on husbandry and
household management.[62]

The Claudes were regulars at Martineau's eccentric evenings. In
London her principles for entertaining had been laid down:

> My rooms were too small for personages who required
> space for display and such were not therefore invited.
> A gentleman who expected a sofa all to himself, while
> a crowd of adorers simpered in his face, was no guest
> for a simple evening party…nor for another who hung
> her white hand over the arm of her chair, and lectured
> metaphysically and sentimentally about art, to the
> annoyance of true connoisseurs…All I ventured upon
> was…a very choice assembly of guests who did not mind
> a little crowding for the sake of the conversation they
> afforded each other.[63]

For a woman such as Jane, now reaching her late twenties and
worrying that her youth was passing, such evenings must have been
beacons in a wintry world often devoid of amusing or interesting
visitors. The sociability came with a price however, Martineau hurling
demands, such as 'O! do find me a cook…' for Jane Arrowsmith,
Martineau's trusted servant and assistant in mesmerism (a form of
hypnotism and healing), was about to leave for Australia.[64] Emigration

was in the air, as Jane knew, for her brother Louis too was preparing to leave, for the USA.

★

Jane was involved, from the late 1840s, in several overlapping teaching projects in Ambleside. Contributing to a twice-weekly evening charity school for forty to fifty local working-class girls, some of them servants, she appears also to have helped at the local National School. These state-supported but not yet free schools were typically attended by the children of tradesmen, shopkeepers and farmers. She, her sister Mary and her mother also taught their little cousins by marriage, the Fells, and they took one or two boarding pupils, some through contacts in Valparaiso.

Jane shared her school teaching with an unusually well-informed group of women including Annie Clough, and the Arnold women: Mrs Arnold, her daughters Mary (Mrs Twining), and Jane who later married W.E. Forster. A Quaker and Liberal MP, he was to be largely responsible for the introduction of free, universal education in England and Wales. In the evening school, Jane taught writing (using poetry), and was the

> purveyor of the music and [I] delight them with such things as Mrs Hemans' Better Land, which I write out in a clear hand and make them copy for themselves at home…[65] I shall have to give up my fancy for a little sociability and ease and the numbers are rather too large for it to act. I am the Louis Napoleon of the school as I have seized on the supreme power to prevent Mrs Watson the national schoolmistress from having it…Mrs Twining and Miss Clough are both too gentle to think of standing at the head of a large room and making a harangue – so I am prince president.[66]

It is through Annie Clough's journal that Jane comes to life during this Ambleside period. Both Annie and Arthur had to support themselves following their father's business collapse and subsequent

27

death in 1844.[67] In Liverpool, at their modest house in Vine Street, Annie spent considerable time and effort on her own learning of mathematics, German, and Latin. And, guided by Arthur, she read contemporary literature including Emmerson, Carlyle, and Martineau's *Deerbrook* (on governesses), and *The Hour and the Man* (on Toussaint L'Ouverture and slavery).

Encouraged by Arthur to move closer to the middle-class market for financial reasons, Annie established her own school in 1852 at Eller How near Ambleside, having gone 'scholar-hunting' among the local trades-people with Mrs Claude to introduce her.[68] Families that could not afford reputable private schools, were in the mid-nineteenth century ill-served in a murky world of small establishments. However, such schools did provide opportunities for unmarried women to support themselves, though generally in inferior conditions to those of the National Schools.[69]

Jane disliked the crude didacticism of many contemporary textbooks, deriding a 'horrid little [German] book in which John asks Bill to steal an apple but Bill said no – which was right John or Bill? & this sort of thing over and again, enough to sicken anyone.'[70] The Claudes kept a great cupboard of toys for parties, and Annie Clough remarked that they excelled in amusing children.[71] Jane could be scornful of the lazy – the affluent Holt boys from Liverpool, summering in Windermere, were 'stupid harmless looking creatures – that neither fish nor climb nor sketch nor row nor walk nor ride.'[72] On the other hand, she was moved by children whose lives were difficult: when away, she asked after the welfare of an Ambleside girl who:

> has been knocked about and made to earn her bread instead of being sent to school…I got her mistress to allow her to come to my Thursday night class and very happy she was to attend…In winter the class assembled at 5 after dark but down she came from Strawberry Bank in sleet and snow and went back again at 7 in the dark…her great clogs like skates.[73]

On a visit to Ireland, Jane's keen eye had noted that:

Irish babies are generally the best off in a family, wearing something more like garments than their elder brothers & sisters – who are draped and festooned after the manner of scarecrows in England. Besides their own little frocks you may see a baby now and then additionally protected by a waistcoat of its father's – A particular friend of mine in the village here – who answers to the name of Dan O'Connel and is 6 or 7 years old – wears ragged girls petticoats tied round his waist – then the upper part of his body is covered by a tippet or two much too large for him – crossed over the chest – and fastened under one arm leaving an open space for the little hand and arm to be thrust in for purposes which shall be nameless. He is the sharpest most impertinent little fellow that ever cheered from a bundle of rags – he is very devoted to me since I promised him a sixpence – which I believe he will not get as it depends on his reading a certain page of a certain book without spelling – He comes every now and then to the door to try and…and calls out "If you please, Miss Jane, here's Dan O'Connel".[74]

Dan O'Connel was the Irish equivalent of the 'dirty children' Jane had encountered while charity visiting and Sunday school teaching in the Liverpool slums. These were the children – and more than twenty thousand were said to run wild on the streets around the docks – so tattered, malnourished and unruly that only the ragged schools would take them. This was a problem that worsened as more and more people were drawn, especially from Ireland, to Liverpool as the main emigration port during the 1840s.[75]

For women such as Jane, involvement in schemes to assist impoverished mothers, or teaching children in Sunday or charity schools, could provide a precious escape from a chaperoned world in which spinster daughters were expected to put relatives' needs before their own.[76] Although Annie Clough recorded a long talk with Jane about 'it being right in certain cases to quit even one's father and mother and family for work as well as for a husband,' Jane, now pushing thirty, was still at her mother's beck and call.[77]

9 *Jane Cannan: 'View in Prahran'. Jane liked children; she had observed 'dirty' and ragged children in Liverpool and Ireland, and encouraged friendless working children to come to the Ambleside school where she taught. This drawing of the area she was to move to in Melbourne shows more than buildings, tents, and tradesmen with horses and carts. A woman feeds poultry and young children tend goats. (Royal Historical Society of Victoria)*

★

Mrs Claude's demanding journeys, however, had their rewards. In Antrim in northern Ireland Jane enjoyed the new crazes for geology – inspecting the Giant's Causeway's basalt columns, 'botanising', and collecting marine specimens. While this was to lead to the denuding of rock pools in some areas, such activities at least alleviated middle class women's boredom and got them outside. Perhaps Jane, like the seaweed expert Margaret Gatty, 'laid aside all thought of conventional appearances', wearing boy's shooting boots, petticoats above the ankle, and old hats rather than bonnets.[78]

The Claude party included the daughter of their father's former business partner, who, as Jane noted, 'adores the state of old maid'. Jane told her cousin Jeannette

> If you could only see Miss Pearson you would give up the notion for ever that English people must be commonplace – she is so quaint sometimes – and always busy – whether she is grubbing up sea weeds with Mary – studying maps of Ireland with Mamma or quarrelling with me for we two are always quarrelling – my victory generally depends on my making her laugh so that she is speechless – You would have stared if you had seen her – a long, tall, stooping slender somewhat large featured individual...At home she is an enthusiastic gardener – & physics all the poor people's children, attends the schools, writes poetry and studies sciences – her bedroom is hung round with ghastly curiosities – and pickled lizards & vipers stand on the chimney piece. A tiny little bed stands like an afterthought up along side of the wall...& at midnight in winter she may be found there cooking herself some arrowroot over her fire & stirring it with a tooth brush handle. [79]

During the winter of 1850-51 Mrs Claude and Jane were in Berlin among their extended family. Jane's hopes for drawing classes and university lectures were however disappointed in an atmosphere of establishment fear and reaction following the 1848 revolutions which had swept Europe. And her German did not flow:

> To my horror find myself almost as shy as I was 7 years ago – I thought I had outgrown or out lived that torment of my youth but I find that I only covered it in England with a rattling style of conversation which made people laugh – here deprived of that weapon by my ignorance of the language I stand like a poor lost sheep and I do not get on at all.[80]

The Claudes returned in time for the Great Exhibition, which proclaimed Britain's place as workshop, banker, clearing house and carrier of the world. Unprecedented numbers from all sections of society travelled to Hyde Park in London, often by special chartered trains, sharing the novelty of public lavatories.[81] The spectacular and elegant Crystal Palace, which housed the exhibition, was constructed of glass and iron and brilliantly exemplified prefabrication.[82] It demonstrated a quick response was possible to rising demand for warehouses as trade expanded, for stabling, stores and accommodation in military campaigns, and for emigrants' and civil servants' housing in colonial settlement and administration.

We don't know Jane's or Mrs Claude's responses to the enormous exhibition, but can suppose that they enjoyed the fine arts section. Did they also look at the nugget of gold from California and wonder how Uncle Charles was getting on in Chile and reflect on the premature death of Uncle Adolphe which had caused the return to England of his family? As Mrs Claude had enjoyed scientific experiments and lectures in Liverpool and Jane had been impressed by Manchester cotton mills, they may have braved the crowds for the noisy machinery section. Perhaps Jane glanced at McConnel's prize-winning corrugated iron railway carriages. Or at Morewood & Rogers' exhibits of corrugated iron roofing sheets, iron tiles, fencing, rainwater goods and other building products, and their model farmyard and buildings, together with agricultural implements, all manufactured from patent galvanised tinned iron, little dreaming that soon she would be drawing such buildings in their destinations.[83] And perhaps she wondered what it would be like to live in Andrew Whytock's one-fourth size model of an emigrant's house described in the Exhibition Catalogue as

> made of Morewood & Rogers' patent galvanised tinned iron, corrugated. The full size weighs about half a ton, and can be packed in two cases…It may be erected by two persons in as many days. Furniture of the house made chiefly of the same material. Table and chairs with camp legs. Bath, answering to the purpose of a sofa, or a bedstead.[84]

One imagines that Jane's brother Louis, waiting for a ship to Philadelphia, found vindication for his decision to become an engineer as he stood before the giant steam locomotive the *Liverpool*, built by his old foundry Bury, Curtis & Kennedy.[85] Science and technology were now centre-stage rather than imprisoned in the grimy, smoky, noisy, northern towns which genteel southerners affected to despise. Greatly impressed by the building itself, Louis returned twice 'to get over the soul bewildering sensation of so many articles all demanding attention at once.'[86]

★

Jane's life then was busy, and not always agreeably so as she told her friend Mary Cannan:

> Jeannette will have told you about the private theatricals and Miss Martineau's regret that she had only one skull to leave for the benefit of science; also that she goes to Birmingham on the 31st to study some manufactures to describe for Dickens' Household Words…the Forsters, arrived yesterday to spend Christmas at Fox How and Matthew (Arnold) and his bride are expected also from Birmingham, where he has been Inspecting schools (I can hardly fancy it)… My Mamma was in bed one day this week with a violent unaccountable headache, and poor Mrs Clough in Liverpool has had eleven teeth out preparatory to clearing the way for an entire artificial set…Miss Clough cannot come to see us this Christmas, as she has several relations in different directions to appease.[87]

While there were 'wet days when Mamma begins to "tidy" and Mary loses her faith in human nature', Broadlands was bearable'.[88] Nevertheless, a restlessness enters Jane's correspondence with Mary Cannan. Although she had intended working on her art, 'I have quarrelled with the lithographing, the stone lies there reproachfully but I cannot set to work'.[89] She read Mrs Gaskell's *Mary Barton* which controversially showed Manchester from the working-class point of view, and wept over *Uncle Tom's Cabin* in which 'there were good and bad masters, good & bad slaves – it was not too one sided.'[90] She envied Mary Cannan 'poking about studios' and could 'imagine herself in a frenzy' about Rome.[91]

In 1852 Jane turned thirty, well beyond the general Victorian age of marriage. Her letters to Mary Cannan contain detailed observations on households and relationships. She had firm friends who were satisfied with the spinster state – Annie Clough, Harriet Martineau, Mary Cannan and Sophy Pearson. But Jane loved children and around her matches were taking place. Jeannette, so much younger, had a suitor in a Berlin cousin, the scientist Emil du Bois Raymond.[92] Arthur Clough had become engaged.

Jane enjoyed staying with Mrs Clough and Annie in Liverpool, and walking down bustling Bold Street, albeit dressed in mourning following the sudden death of her guardian James Brancker. She described the old family friends the Doerings, he a German sugar merchant from Java:

> Another day Mrs D. says "Doering will you pay this bill for me tomorrow" – M – says he, send Fred; Oh Doering – you are not so amiable as I thought but no matter we have only been married 20 years, perhaps in 20 more I shall have <u>arranged</u> you quite to my satisfaction – This tickled me amazingly – Mrs D <u>arranges</u> everything from her tea table to her children's teeth and her husband…Mrs D. is very good hearted but rather apt to take up things very warmly and then cool – one day we met a clergyman to whom she bowed – then said to me – "Dear me I have so many left off clergymen – I can hardly stir for them; and so it is; she is always very much admiring some clergyman and sending all the children to be influenced by him.[93]

And then there was the compromise made by Jane's friend Jane Cooper in marrying 'Old Raven', a widowed clergyman with his habit of 'paternally and clerically kissing all the young ladies'.[94] Fortunately, during a visit, there was time alone to chat, Jane Cooper curling Jane's front hair for her ('how are the mighty fallen!'):

> Jane says she likes the old thing well enough but they appear to have had a few tiffs in their married life…they go on like two babies. At dinner she says – if you will have a glass of sherry – I will – he replies – and if I won't what then? – Why I will <u>still</u> says she…He has a sweet gentle voice, which must have helped him to her favour – but he is not so liberal as I thought – He calls Miss Martineau a fool…and has no patience with roman catholics & does not allow his children to go to theatres or operas – can't bear the name of Carlyle.[95]

Not a meeting of minds, then. On the other hand, Jane's friend and artist Augusta Wotherspoon's recent marriage, only made possible when her father suddenly died, presented a more intriguing image. There had been general disapproval of her suitor Mr Migault – why is not clear – was he a radical, extravagant, argumentative, or just poor? He got his living in Liverpool by tutoring in German and perhaps other subjects, and Jane had known him, through long-standing Berlin family connections, all her life.[96] At any rate, once married, the Migaults went to Tübingen where he worked on his doctorate. Living frugally in small but sunny lodgings and taking their meals in cafés, all for a pittance compared to English prices, they were 'undeniably happy'.[97]

This simple, friendly, bohemian marriage offered a vision of a partnership free of Victorian domestic stiffness, of the making of antimacassars and tablemats, and the placating of relatives. Jane had survived the loneliness of Berlin by confiding in Mary Cannan. Perched in her Tarpeian Rock lodgings in Rome, she was now acting as a go-between.

THREE

A timid kiss and talk of corrugated iron

- *Iron Houses for California &c manufactured by Mr John Walker (son of the original patentee) at his corrugated iron works. Agent Robert Wrighton, Liverpool.* (Liverpool Mercury, *19 February 1850*)
- *Lime Street Station roofed in galvanised corrugated iron.* (Liverpool Mercury, *22 February 1850*)
- *A corrugated iron lighthouse, with wrought iron piles and iron girders, constructed by Mr J. Walker for Florida, exhibited in London.* (Daily News, *1 February 1851*)
- *E. T. Bellhouse – Iron ballroom for Balmoral – as a result of his model iron house at the Great Exhibition, of Eagle Foundry, Manchester.* (Morning Chronicle, *1 September 1851*)
- *Iron church for mariners at Cardiff completed in 2 weeks.* (Bristol Mercury, *7 August 1852*)
- *Railway station built in Birmingham for Rio de Janeiro.* (Morning Chronicle, *13 September, 1852*)

Following the discovery of gold in 1851 in Australia's newly created colony of Victoria, businesses jostled to meet the burgeoning demand for housing and commercial buildings. Morewood & Rogers do not feature much in the many pages of British newspaper advertisements

ADMIT · TO THE SERVICE IN
the first PORTABLE CHURCH, *Built for the Diocese of* MELBOURNE,
at the Manufactory. CLIFT HOUSE, BRISTOL.
3 O'Clock Friday 13ᵗʰ May 1853.

10 *Invitation to a service in a Hemming church in Bristol before its dispatch to Melbourne. There was enormous public interest in the prefabricated iron buildings and eight hundred tickets were issued for this service. Once gold was discovered near Melbourne, fear of vice among the diggers provoked a spate of church exports. (Bristol Reference Library)*

directed at would-be merchants and emigrants, perhaps because they were already in a strong position, holding several patents. They were well established in New York, probably supplying zinc wire and other products for telegraph lines as well as roofing, and their iron tiles, known as Morewood's Patent Galvanized Tinned Plates, had been exported to Natal in South Africa from 1850. Henry Palmer's invention in 1829 of the corrugation of wrought iron sheets, by passing them through rollers, had increased the roofing possibilities. Galvanising with zinc to prevent corrosion heralded an era in which light and strong mass-produced materials made possible (it was claimed) termite and fire-proof buildings. Morewood & Rogers had galvanising works in Stratford in east London, together with works in Wolverhampton and Birmingham, but in the main they operated though a contract with Walker's Gospel Oak Mill at Tipton in Staffordshire.[98] In Australia, their principal agency was at Adelaide, doing reasonable business in a region underpinned by copper mining and wool. There were also Morewood & Rogers agents or correspondents in Sydney, Swan River, Launceston and Hobart.[99]

★

Margaret Cannan, the mother of Jane's friend Mary Cannan, was born a Kennedy. Her uncle was a Manchester cotton magnate, John Kennedy, one of the stream of Scottish engineers who nourished the industrial revolution in the north of England. After his apprenticeship to William Cannan in Lancashire, training as an engineer in cotton machine-making, Kennedy had set up business with James McConnel, moving into the fabulously prosperous trade of cotton spinning. These inter-related lowland Scots created a firm, whose 'mills, like gorgeous palaces, arise and lift their useful turrets to the skies!'; it became Manchester's largest in this field, its fine yarn in demand in Switzerland, Germany and France as well as in Ireland and throughout Britain.[100]

Mary Cannan was David's older sister by seven years. She had stronger memories than he of their austere infancy and childhood in the Presbyterian manse at Carsphairn in the remote Galloway hills in the south west of Scotland, and of their educated, handsome, frustrated and consumptive father the Reverend Thomas Cannan. When he died in 1832, the widowed Margaret Cannan took her young children to Galloway's coastal town of Kirkcudbright and enrolled them at its Academy, relatives and a church charity helping with the fees. Mary, already a prolific reader with a gift for languages, was a favourite with the school-masters who turned a blind eye to her refusal to sew with the girls.[101] Practical Mrs Cannan placed David and his brothers in the commercial section of the school, where David won prizes for arithmetic. There was a modicum of classics and literature eagerly absorbed by the Cannan children who were buoyed by memories of their father's erudition, and of uncle James Cannan – renowned for his love of learning and thrift (and for his ability to recognise sheeps' faces) – who farmed at The Shiel, the ancestral Cannan estate since the sixteenth century.

Mrs Cannan's uncle, John Kennedy, lived at Ardwick Hall in Manchester, and here her first cousins had been born. These women had married within the tightly integrated world of nonconformist, Liberal Manchester manufacturing: Margaret married Henry McConnel, Elizabeth married John Greg (connecting the Kennedys with the Greg cotton dynasty originally at Quarry Bank), Annis married Albert Escher of Zurich (presumably an agent of McConnel & Co's; she later became Mrs James Heywood M.P.), Mary married Samuel Robinson, and Rachel married Edwin Chadwick who moved to London where he pursued his public health campaigns.

Mrs Cannan used these cousins to secure employment for her seven children. During the 1840s her daughters Agnes and Margaret became governesses in the John Greg household in Lancaster, and Mary in the William Rathbone Greg household in Ambleside. Mrs Cannan's sons, perhaps favoured as John Kennedy had only one son, worked as clerks in Manchester businesses associated with Kennedy and McConnel.

The contrast between the 'distressed' and the wealthy Scots cousins may not have been as great as we imagine: conspicuous displays of wealth were yet to supersede plainness among the nonconformist business class. The affluent cotton masters' families at that time were pioneering a distinctive, bourgeois way of life and outlook. These were not the cultural philistines later caricatured by Matthew Arnold, using, as they did, their wealth for civic schemes in the shape of parks, reading rooms, mechanics' institutes, statistical societies, bathhouses and infirmaries.[102]

David started as an accounts clerk, rising to a responsible position, with McConnel & Co (as the original partnership became known) until his health broke down, probably through chronic bronchitis, at the age of twenty-three. After recovering in Kircudbrightshire, he moved to London in 1851, to assist Edwin Chadwick in drawing up plans for London's urgently needed extramural cemeteries.[103] McConnel's reference written for Chadwick stated that David was 'clear-headed and exact in accounts', and was trustworthy, honest '& of correct habits of life'.[104] However, David soon shifted to Morewood & Rogers. In another illustration of the usefulness of extended family ties, Edmund Morewood's sister was married to the younger James McConnel, David's second cousin, who, as David said, was always kind and 'got me my present shop'.[105]

Morewood & Rogers' London office was at the Steel Yard Wharf on Upper Thames Street, in the area near St Paul's. We can imagine David in the labyrinthine streets of the Dickensian City of London, among legions of clerks and book-keepers in black frock-coats and stove-pipe hats. Elegant, airy Georgian and Regency squares and thoroughfares to the west of the City contrasted with the old commercial heart of London stretching eastwards along the stinking cesspool of the Thames, 'a city which was covered by a patina of fog and decay, a city which simply had no resources for those who poured into its dens and courtyards.'[106] David, recently so ill that he had been unable to speak, would not have found much change from smoky Manchester. London's half a million coal fires regularly combined with industrial smoke to create noxious muddy brown fogs that enveloped everything in a choking, sulphurous gloom. No wonder Chadwick lost him to Morewood & Rogers, who, prompted by their Adelaide agent Andrew Pollock to respond to the discoveries of 'gold more or less all over the place', were considering opportunities in Melbourne.

★

Over this period Jane found a new freedom in chaperoning her eighteen-year-old cousin Jeannette around Manchester and Liverpool. A sense of playfulness pervades Jane's many hasty notes to her. Jane enjoyed advising on books to read, popular preachers to hear, and cotton mills to marvel at, and she treated Jeannette as an assistant in the schools she was involved in. Jeannette was an outlet for Jane's pent-up affections; a very clever young woman, fluent in several languages, she was nevertheless curiously insular, a trait Jane identified with. Martineau had reservations, hinting at a selfish streak in her character, telling Jane that 'it was wonderful that a younger person should have such influence over the older, and gave me to understand that she thought my views of things would be far juster than Jeannette's'.[107]

In 1852 Jane's letters become coyly conspiratorial. David had stayed at Broadlands, a visit arranged by his sisters Agnes and Margaret, and Jeannette had called at the Cannans' home at Elm Terrace in Manchester, where David's brother

> James seems to have frightened her by asking "sudden questions", Tom to have interested her without the intervention of speech – and David to have protected her and finally seen her home and promised to take her over a

mill – I gave her a strict charge not to cut me out – but I feel a little nervous on the subject.[108]

James was the same age as Jane, working in a bank and probably dreaming of the time when he would become a well-read drama critic for the *Manchester City News*. His vivacity, however, was flawed, and perhaps evidently so to Jane, by a belief that the Cannans were more remarkable than other people. James was at once scornful and generous, tolerant and bigoted, with a weakness for whisky when disappointment crept into life.[109]

David shared some of these characteristics, masked as a Carlylean contempt for cant, hypocrisy, and vested interests. James, though, may not have been the only Scot to feel 'different' and more remarkable than the general population in England. This mind-set, overlapping with Presbyterian non-conformism (and Unitarianism), allowed an educated man, however poor, to consider himself a gentleman, for earthly distinctions were irrelevant to God. It gave men who had not been raised in sophisticated circumstances (as in Carlyle's own life) a confidence in entering society – for, whether religiously or politically-speaking, pomp and conventions were unimportant. Such social confidence is also a feature of the Huguenot Claudes – well-educated but not from the 'best' schools, nor living in grand houses, nor able to afford more than a minimally respectable wardrobe. In both Scottish and Huguenot societies, people of different status were typically bound together because worth rested more in conduct, and especially industriousness and self-betterment, and less in birth. In short the Claudes and Cannans shared the cultural capital of being well-read and self-disciplined, with a disdain for rank and worldliness.[110]

From Stockport, near Manchester, and on her way to Hastings for a tour of duty with the Ravens, Jane reported to Jeannette that

Agnes insisted on sending David word to meet me at the London Station – and [the Cannans] all invited me to stay there when I came back – they took me to the train – James

42

was quite surprised at my being capable – of having left my luggage at the right station on the way to their house – and when I was going in the carriage & showed my ticket when it was required of me – I heard him say to Agnes – "<u>Upon my word</u> quite independent"![111]

All at once, Jane dropped into a disjointed letter to Jeannette that she felt in a great panic:

We discussed so much about "waiting"…two years is a good round time to keep people quiet with – and it may be either shorter or longer as circumstances turn out…Before I forget business – Miss Clough wants a back comb – a buffalo horn one to hold up her back hair …No one I believe, not even David himself knows how much I love him…I am sure I hardly know myself – Ever your affectionate Jane Claude. I don't like the look of Jane Dorothea Cannan but I glory in Mrs David Cannan – does that not look well?[112]

By mid 1852, then, David Cannan and Jane had an undeclared engagement. In November Jane reported to Mary Cannan that her correspondence with him was flourishing:

I have as many different thoughts about the matter as there are days in the week or moods in my Gemüt [nature] so that there is not much use telling what I think today – I have written so much that I begin to wonder whether I shall be able to answer for it when I do see him – and he writes so much nonsense that I sometimes think he never means a word he says – but if he ever said half of the teasing complimentary things in earnestness and seriousness I should be the proudest and happiest of Janes – though I should have the misgiving that it could not be for <u>his</u> good, and that you and Agnes were very bad sisters to him to let him come to Broadlands…

Miss Martineau has invited me to the wedding breakfast of her maid Martha on the 22nd [December] and I must stay for that – did I tell you about it – Martha is to marry a Mr Andrews – master of the Ragged Schools at Bristol – and Mr [Philip] and Miss [Mary] Carpenter from there are coming to Miss M's for the occasion as Martha is sister to the farming man, Fulcher he and his wife will be of the party – Susan Arnold and I are invited – and I suppose some friends of Martha's from the village – it will be a strange mixture…but I admire her much for being so pleased with Martha's prospects that she never says a word of her own loss – which is more serious as Jane [Arrowsmith] the other favourite maid has just gone to Australia…poor Miss M. must fall in to the hands of strangers.[113]

The 'strange mixture' of wedding guests – the Carpenter family who were eminent Unitarian reformers and teachers, local gentry, and farming people and servants – made real Martineau's principle that servants should be respected rather than treated as little more than serfs. In Martineau's own account of the occasion, she describes how she told the bride that:

it would be a convenience and pleasure to me if she would be my guest in the sitting-room for the few days before the marriage…The evening before, when Mr Carpenter delivered a Temperance lecture, Miss [Mary] Carpenter and I sent the entire household to the lecture; and we set out the long table for the morning, dressed the flowers (which came from neighbouring conservatories) and put on all the cold dishes; covered the whole and shut up the cat.[114]

★

Emil du Bois Raymond had visited England during that summer of 1852. Whether Jeannette felt happy and excited we do not know, but she was making a 'good' match, for Emil was rich and clever, and destined to become an eminent Berlin physiologist. The cousins' engagements provoked jocular letters. Playing on the fact that she and Jeannette were both J. Claude, Jane wrote:

> My dear Emil,
>
> I was taken by surprise the other day. I read that you were engaged to me. I was quite delighted – for I always thought it was a mistake your taking that little…inferior cousin of mine – who is really too young and…too insignificant…to be united to a reputation such as yours – now however – I see it all – and admire the cleverness with which you led us all astray – <u>in order to spare my feelings</u>, as for the poor child herself – she will soon get over the disappointment – it was only the other day that she said she would rather have a poor miserable scotchman of our acquaintance <u>because he slept under nine blankets.</u>
>
> So you see <u>she</u> is beneath contempt – her mother perhaps will be a little vexed, but it is far better than if it had not been found till after the wedding – It would have been such an expense sending us back & forward, as even she is too heavy to go by post. I hope you like Italy, of course you will continue writing to Jeannette it is much pleasanter for me – and saves me postage and the trouble of answering the letters, which is a consideration as I don't write german fluently – or so well as she. Perhaps I had better give her the Scotchman's address & she could go direct from here so as not to lose time. [115]

And Louis sent Jeannette word from America that if he had had any idea 'that she wished to marry a cousin he would have offered himself, trusting his cousinship would cover a multitude of sins.' His heart in fact was elsewhere, pursuing a colleague's sister, Elvira Ward. In a break from the discomforts of railroad surveying in Kentucky's virgin forests he had met her family in New York, sleeping in a comfortable bedroom for the first time in ten months.[116]

Impatient with 'worldly' concerns over dress and appearance, and with what Louis referred to as 'pomps and vanities', Jane disappointed a prettily-dressed Agnes Cannan who was staying with her at Broadlands:

> I am afraid I could not let her "get me up" – my mission is not to wear roses…but I did think I was a little improved since I have fallen into the hands of a dressmaker who has inspired me with such confidence that as long as the garments were only wide enough and moderately long [she] was allowed to do what she pleased – As for the curls – Jeannette seemed to have a pride in having as much influence over me as Mrs Raven – and left me in fear till they were all swept away again…Miss Martineau will again throw up her eyes in despair – and say why on earth don't you please yourself?[117]

Dashing about the country on her errands, Jane took pains to cross paths with David in London. Mrs Chadwick ('all that her husband Edwin was not – charming, witty, with a great sense of fun'[118]) seems to have acted as a meeting point, as she did for Jeannette and Emile. On one occasion, Jane wrote to Jeannette:

> I go to Mrs Chadwick's on thursday & foolishly said I would be there at three – thinking the whole morning too long for her – I wrote such a stupid note to her that I blush whenever I think of it. I also wrote so stupidly to David Cannan – that the chances are he keeps away on thursday and does not come to the Chadwicks, as was the original intention…Such is life I feel as if thursday would never come.[119]

And there was yet another service to perform on arriving back in Ambleside:

Mary Cannan's little German translation has arrived at last and to Miss Martineau's horror it has been written on <u>both sides of the sheet</u> – which is an abomination in the eyes of all printers. Miss M is rather cool and crusty about the affair altogether and evidently does not like the business so this annoyed her – "hardly any publisher would look at it written in that way" – Of course you guess what I said. I said Give it to me and I will write it beautifully in a week…I began last night & though at the utmost verge of my endurance through making mistakes and wasting two beautifully written sheets I got through a good deal last night – It seems such a shame to waste all the beautiful writing and it is a sad bore to me to keep my eye on all the semi colons and apostrophes – but I shall get used to that – and will have a fire in the dining room & work five hours a day.[120]

★

It was Jane's involvement in an extraordinary collapse of a marriage that clinched her relationship with David. A Mrs Lewis ran a small girls' boarding school at her home, Belmont, in Guildford in Surrey. The previous autumn, Jane had been assisting there, 'in high favour with Dr Lewis on account of the curls', but now Jane returned to smooth over a 'blow-up' of his sanity. [121] Having to contain him at home, Mrs Lewis told Jane when David called that they would have to walk by themselves – "no one knows either of you here, and you can either go to church or walk as you find the weather turns out". Jane questioned 'whether David Cannan knows that it is not customary for young ladies & gentlemen to walk out alone on Sunday afternoons, but be that as it may – he did not seem much alarmed for his character, and we went a beautiful walk…where there is a ruin and a splendid view'. When the magistrates ordered him to leave the house, Dr Lewis claimed that

it was only a "habit" he had of clenching his fists – and that threatening to wring her neck was only a sort of expression

&c…Poor Mrs Lewis – and all that wicked man could say in his best mood was "Well, well Betsy – never mind – you're a <u>fine</u> woman yet – many women half your age have not your figure!" I groan in the spirit when I think of the life she has led for twenty years – We feel she says like the slaves who got to Canada.[122]

Jane's account to Mary Cannan had included her own, composed attempt to induce some calm into the situation before David's arrival:

On New Year's Day [Dr Lewis] broke out so violent that I was terrified – he followed Mrs Lewis about the house with clenched fists, went down on his knees to curse her and used such shocking language – and said such shocking things of me…Meanwhile I from habit – made no observation but sat stitching away at my work waiting for an interval to ask some question about politics or the theory of the Tides.[123]

Walking on their own again, David and Jane crossed the boundary. To Jeannette she wrote:

He is really & truly transformed into my David – and I am his own dear Jane and the hope and joy of his life & the delight of his heart…he was so quiet & calm that it did me good to look at him – but there will be room for patience to be tried for he says it will be two or even three years before he can see me any where "but in cabs, railway stations – or hotels with Mrs Jacksons".[124]

Mary Cannan heard from Jane that David

after giving me one timid gentle kiss, has talked a whole Sunday afternoon about corrugated iron and things in general....He was...so benevolent to Miss Maddison the new teacher that we were all happy together round the fire and did not mind the wet afternoon which cheated us of our walk...

They pity me at home [over the Lewis situation]...for they do not know what has been going on meanwhile between me and David and have no idea...of the three letters I carry in my pocket, and read at all odd moments to decide which is the nicest...

How much I owe to you of my happiness – it is not only that you have been the means of bringing us together with minds duly prepared to appreciate each other – but if I had not had you in Berlin to pour my whole soul out before I should have been very different now – and though a little qualm comes over me sometimes, I do feel as if I could make David as happy as extraneous circumstances can make people, but that is because he is so good and industrious – and so ready to sympathize with all human beings and not one to expect me to be perfection...

Dear Mary do you know that this April, the three years, which I solemnly devoted to Mamma and Mary are over, and now comes the new work – the best work it seems.[125]

David's poor health was the cloud over the happiness. He had much in common with Jane – both outsiders in England, both had lost fathers in early childhood, both grew up in educated, thrifty households. While Jane's asides at those who gave themselves airs were gentler than his sarcastic dismissals, for now he softened, adding into Jane's letter to Mary that he thought himself 'so fortunate and love her so much and I am sure I have good reason, have not I?' Jane was fully aware of his frailty, of his thinness and

a jaw that seems almost to cut through the skin – you must remind me that if he is to be ill that I can nurse him all the

Parsonage House for the Diocese of Melbourne, South Australia.

11 Jane knew she would live in a Morewood & Rogers iron house.
Perhaps she envisaged something like this spacious Hemming parsonage,
advertised in English newspapers, with its sitting room, kitchen,
servants' room, stores and pantry. Hemming's houses were usually
timber framed, with walls and roof of corrugated iron, and insulated
with felt. (Bristol Reference Library)

better for my 30 years and my grey hair – and that if he
never lives to be old – it is a more precious trust to be the
hope and joy of a short life than a long one – you must not
wonder at my being serious, happiness makes one so – and
gives one thoughts of death.[126]

But despite this, he was rather dashing. Daguerreotypes taken at
this time show a direct and somewhat arrogant gaze, large eyes (with
heavy shadows beneath them), straight sandy hair falling across the
forehead and over the ears, a generous mouth and a high forehead.
Surely, Jane could cautiously think of life and its blessings.

FOUR

Radiantly happy and many weeping goodbyes

> **PORTABLE HOMES** *To a casual observer, passing up or down the Thames, the Isle of Dogs exhibits at the present moment the aspect of a newly discovered colony having extensive gold regions in its immediate vicinity. Temporary erections, principally galvanised tinned iron, arise to-day like mushrooms which to-morrow are unbolted, unscrewed, and packed in the smallest possible space for portions of the globe almost immediately under our feet. Curious enough that the mother country, after all, should provide homes for the emigrant from her shores, and from what we have seen today, through the courtesy of Messrs Morewood and Rogers, of the Steel Yard, [Upper] Thames Street, not only is the small shed the private dwelling of two to twelve rooms, with every appliance of English comfort to be had "by order", but warehouses, factories, and even foundries are equally subject in a tariff of so much per foot.* (The Standard, *12 May 1853*)

In 1853 news reached Britain of desperate housing shortages in Victoria. What was shocking was not that labourers in their thousands, but that merchants, farmers, artisans, members of the middle-classes, might be at best be in tents, at worst were wandering the streets with their wives and families.[127] The need for quick and simple emigrant housing now focused the minds of manufacturers.

Portable buildings had been sent to Australia since 1788 with the first fleet's canvas cabins and the second fleet's military hospital.[128] During the 1830s Manning had devised an ingenious £15 wooden 'portable colonial cottage', with furnishings packed within each other, 'complete for habitation in a few hours after landing'. The Californian gold-rush of 1849 added impetus to the manufacture of prefabricated wooden houses, which were soon replaced by mass-produced iron structures for a growing number of customers in the Australian and New Zealand markets.[129] The Bristol manufacturer Samuel Hemming's portable houses, evolved from a design for his emigrant son, impressed *The Bristol Mercury*, as 'simple in construction, perfect in arrangement, efficient in character'.[130]

Ingenious packaging, given shipping costs which were based on volume (or compass), was important. A Bristol visitor to the Hemming works was told, seeing a moderate-sized box,

> 'That is the whole of one house, and that bundle braced together is the rafters and principals; and you will observe that the flooring forms the packing-case; the iron clamps at the corners are for the principal, instead of mortise and tenon-joints, which emigrants could not manage; and the whole weight is perhaps under two tons.'[131]

Manufacturers stressed their buildings' flexibility of design (providing a shop front for instance), and the ingenuity with which they were equipped with cooking equipment and furnishings and so forth.[132]

In 1853 Morewood & Rogers took a riverside site on the Isle of Dogs (also known as Millwall) for the display and packing of their buildings for export. Here, among smoky iron foundries, forests of ships' masts and spars, busy local steamers and river traders, was the West India Dock, with vast, austere brick warehouses for rum and sugar. Nearby, John Walker told readers of the

Times classified advertisements, he too had three acres of ground on which examples of his remarkably cheap patent iron houses could be inspected. Hemming was doing the same at his Clift-House works in Bristol, creating an artificial town of stores, churches, houses of various sizes, and shops, that drew large and admiring crowds (see frontispiece). [133]

Morewood & Rogers were assured by Andrew Pollock that Victoria relied less on convict labour than New South Wales, that its settlers tended to be 'hard-working and honourable Scotchmen' and that it had the stability of a established wool market. With the addition of gold its future was secure. Melbourne and Geelong, therefore, needed their own dedicated agent (rather than his continuing to supply both colonies from Adelaide), for profits would far exceed the revenues of South Australia where access to copper riches was limited by often impassable roads. [134]

★

Jane had started 1853 assuming she must wait two or three years for David to earn enough for them to be married, meaning, according to the advice manuals, for people like themselves, an income of around £300 per annum. [135] She described David's position with Morewood & Rogers as 'a trial thing with still Mr Chadwick to fall back upon'. [136] By March, however, David wrote to Mary Cannan that

> Morewood & Rogers made me an offer to go to Australia which was too good to be refused so I accepted & am going to take Jane with me…I am in excellent spirits first in getting Jane so much sooner than I expected & secondly at going to Australia…
>
> I am not sure whether we shall go eventually to Melbourne or to Adelaide but we go to Melbourne first. There is an establishment at both places & they are at present conducted by one man; if we divide them I am to have one third of the profits and if we keep them as one I am to have one sixth − but if my share in the profits does

not amount to £300 a year I am to have that sum paid me,
however I expect to make more than that or else I shall do
very badly...

I spent yesterday with Mrs Chadwick – Mr C is quite
well again and full of Australia and was very civil and kind
– Mrs C very congratulatory of course – She [and I] were
at the theatre the other night – we went to see Macbeth,
which was well got up but I confess I thought more about
finding a good ship.[137]

Jane's letter shortly before Easter to Jeannette fretted over the
many friends she had to see before her departure, characteristically
dismissing any wedding smartness

by refusing white muslin & orange flowers – but I have
not bettered myself much – for "they" will not let me have
anything thick & comfortable...I have secured a straw
bonnet, but of course if it can be trimmed into any degree
of whiteness – & with a dress of some delusory silvery grey
barege-gauze sort of substance I shall just be as much out
of my element as in white. Then they will make me have a
white muslin cape instead of a black silk one – so if I could
be made miserable by dress – I would – but I am quite
resigned and philosophical.[138]

To David's sister Agnes Jane wrote from Liverpool of her mother
and aunt adapting Jeannette's beautiful undergarments for her amid
a great bustle of things to get done:

I could not have believed that I could have left home so
comfortably as I am doing...Mamma too is pretty cheerful
about it and was in such horror at the idea of my being left
here on her hands if [David] went alone – that she thinks it
quite a blessing I can go...I shall write them such cheerful
letters that they will never have the heart to wish me back

– and after all we may come back in a few years – and if
David gets strong and looks like other people no one will
be sorry – I did not say so but I always thought London
would kill him sooner or later and if he gets strong – I shall
want half the credit for taking good care of him – and not
letting him go away by himself.[139]

Martineau, as usual combining business and pleasure, wrote to
Mary Carpenter:

I have just said farewell to my dear Jane Claude, who, with
her lover & several friends, has spent a parting evening here.
She marries this week – a dreadful loss to the sinners &
sufferers of this place, – & to the happy too.[140]

Always keen on emigration, Martineau saw a chance to help Alfred
Webb, the eighteen year-old son of the radical Dublin Quaker printer
Richard Webb, sending him a card of introduction to the Cannans
(see picture no 8).[141] In her note to David she recommended Alfred,
'an excellent youth', clever, and a great reader, though inclined to an
'anxious conscientiousness':

He has his good cousin, William Thompson, with him, so
that Jane & you need not trouble your heads at all about
amusing him, or taking any particular care of him. We should
all be sorry that he should be <u>at all</u> in your way. This is quite
sincere: & I hope you will act accordingly.
My dear love to Jane. I miss her already, & shall more &
more I believe. I wish you & her all possible happiness.[142]

Meanwhile, a marriage settlement had been prepared with Uncle
Charles Claude and Jane's brother Louis the trustees of Jane's assets.
At the time married women could not own property in their own
right, but such settlements gave wives and their children a measure of
financial security.[143] Uncle Charles gave Jane £500; she would receive

the income from this, but would be dependent on others to look after the capital. Problems were stacked up for the future. Nevertheless, for now she had some £25 a year from this sum, as well as her usual allowance from Uncle Charles.[144] This £50 or so a year was far from enough to live on, but it was a substantial cushion.

★

Having no father, David was launched into marriage by his prosperous Kennedy and Greg relations, staying with the John Gregs at Caton near Lancaster. Fatherless Jane was given away by the surgeon William Fell (Tante Minne's husband), travelling to Ambleside's church in carriages with smart yellow jockeys and 'capital horses'. Agnes sent an account of the wedding day to her sister Mary Cannan:

> I must tell you that Jane paid calls in the village from 8 until two o'clock the day before, and many weeping goodbyes… After we had some breakfast I went into Jane's room & helped to dress her with Mrs Claude. She kept very merry telling us "we were a worldly minded set and she was glad to leave us" – Her petticoat was too short & I took off mine and put it on her, her gown was very pretty, a lovely colour and that sort of silky transparent material you have seen handkerchiefs made of, her muslin mantle looked very pretty too, spotted muslin not coming lower than the waist with frills all round – a lovely lace collar and sleeves, a very pretty white bonnet and veil with myrtle inside – She danced after she was dressed.
>
> …When we got to church we found David & James and a gay party from Mrs Adolophe [Claude]'s – Jeannette dressed in blue silk, white opera cloak trimmed with rose colour…The churchyard was filled with gay people & the road lined with children in their best with flowers in their hands.
>
> [We] saw her coming along with Mr Fell speaking to all the children & smiling upon them so cheerily. She smiled

too when she got up to the altar & stood beside David – he looked very much affected but not overcome quite – I did not see any more – As we came out the children strewed the flowers & when we got home we found David & Jane – she said she felt so much the same she thought she must go & have it done over again!

Jane looks so radiantly happy it is more striking in her than in him tho' he looks very beaming at times. The Claudes are very hopeful about his health and Mrs Claude quite hopes to see them back again in a few years. Miss Martineau still very doleful about it I believe – David so delicate she thinks. Jane smiled, some say laughed in church most of the time…I think Jane will like the adventurous life…

After a little we went down to a beautiful tasteful breakfast – all sorts of lovely flowers there must have been a dozen greenhouses robbed at least to do it all…The cake beautiful in the middle ornamented with spring flowers & the turkey & the game fowls jellies blancmanges oysters potted char [trout] &c. – No speeches made but plenty of talk…I don't think I mentioned how pretty the five maids looked in their lilac gowns and white caps as they waited and how well Jane looked as she divided the cake among the Fells…

Everybody kept up to the last – old shoes were thrown & Jane threw them back most heartily. Tom says [he saw] David shaking hands heartily with one of the servants – If I heard it once how often did I hear that David had been a fortunate man, that she was the gem of the valley – All the village had such a look of quiet…sorrowful interest as Mrs Crossfield said "the good wishes of the valley are upon thee" – When she came down to go off she had on her Manchester bonnet (a white straw with bluish ribbons) a black mantle and a drab [light brown] gown…Jane does look a good deal older than David but that is of little importance.[145]

David wrote to his mother from Kirkby Lonsdale, an ancient market town between the Lake District and the Yorkshire Dales, staying in an old-fashioned country inn. Going to church at nearby Casterton, he and Jane saw several hundred of the female scholars from its two schools, one for servants, the other for the daughters of the clergy. This latter school had been, in an earlier incarnation, the model for the bleak Lowood in Charlotte Brontë's *Jane Eyre*.

Margaret and Agnes Cannan subsequently reported that the couple had 'enjoyed themselves very much and had many jokes about the difficulty of ordering dinners and of passing off as old married people, how they always forgot and acquainted one another with their peculiarities before other people.'[146]

★

David and Jane now had three weeks to prepare for Australia. In London they stayed in lodgings at 17 Bryanstone Street, in the elegant Portman estate in London's West End. Jane told her new mother-in-law (who will be distinguished from Jane by referring to her as Mrs Cannan) that she had been exceedingly busy calling on friends.

> I have been also dining alone – as David, who went off first thing this morning to Upper Thames St – said if he was not back at 2 he would not be back till evening – [A] dilemma of our married life is my position at present with a note from Mrs Chadwick in my hands inviting us to dinner at half past 6 this evening!! What <u>do</u> wives do on such occasions – after much fruitless consideration I have come to the determination of going to Mrs Chadwick bodily with the answer, & as it rains really horridly I shall be extravagant enough to go there in a cab so David will know better another time than to leave me at home with full leave to do whatever I like.
>
> We got here very comfortably and the landlady takes every opportunity of Cannanising me – she is very friendly and

12 Jane Cannan: 'Love to her aunt Louise'. Jane drew this English scene for an aunt in Berlin when she was sixteen. Jane had friends in the Welsh border country near Wrexham, where perhaps she sketched. There is already a nostalgia for a quiet, 'natural' rusticity that she was leaving behind and which she was to echo in her drawings of Australian cottages. (Julia Johnson)

sociable and has already confided to me "that Mr Cannan was such a quiet man she could make nothing of him".[147]

To Jeannette she sent more intimate vignettes:

The evening at [David's cousins] the McMillans was well enough if I had not been rather sleepy after the late dinner and if I had not been horrified by seeing my precious husband "Sundrops"!! David Cannan!!! drink toddy actually mix it with hot water and sugar – and drink it – there was both whiskey & gin – and he took gin – when I argued that the whiskey was more gentlemanly than the gin he said it was not so strong and he had chosen it for that reason as he liked neither – So I forgave him this once but he means to have brandy in the cabin miserable deceived deluded woman that I am...

See what it is to be a married woman – my dear – I think it would amuse you more than anything to see David come in when I am getting ready for a walk and put by a brooch and things and shut up the trunk &c that I may get ready quicker – and the same when I was arraying myself in the silk dress to go to the McMillans he insisted on fastening the dress instead of my ringing for the girl and after philosophising about the top hook and remonstrating with me for my habit of shaking myself into my clothes he got gradually down and when it got too low he <u>went on his knees to finish it!</u> He was highly amused at my having left all the brooches but approved of your Mamma's for that occasion and finally pinned down the little valenciennes collar quite neatly and carried my shoes in his pocket...

Yesterday we had to go off from the Waterloo Station at ten – and it is a long way to go – and instead of getting up early and going comfortably we let time slip on till we had hardly time to get any breakfast as usual – he was ready first

& drank the tea – and when I scrambled in for mine I was received with "I say, this is the silliest thing we have done yet" – which amused me so that I could not choke down my piece of bread which was put in a paper and eaten in the cab!!…

[We] occasionally indulge in little impromptu suppers though we profess to take none – You would laugh if you saw us with the loaf between us and saw me using the knife for butter and cleaning it on my bread for him to use for preserves afterwards – and you would guess that he would be the one for turning the loaf down that it might not get dry – They are very particular in this lodging house and assist us to live cheap by always expecting us to do the most saving thing – so I took care not to leave the finery box open lest they should get the idea that I was an heiress.

To neutralise the horror of the toddy I find some good traits in [David] – he does not grind down cabmen and when we come in late and the girl has sat up for us he gives her a shilling – but pray don't comment on all these things lest I find it convenient to hand him your letter.[148]

★

A journey by sea to Australia took an immense amount of organisation. And as Melbourne was both undeveloped and overcrowded with new arrivals, household equipment had to be bought and packed in huge cases with charges for excess amounts. Was it alarming or exciting that among the shipping lines' announcements of ships bound for Australia (and Melbourne in particular), traders offered tents, carts, harness, miners' tools, gold washing cradles, Chubb's safes, boxes with massive bolts, portable beds that folded into chairs, bowie knives, six shot revolvers and muskets with bayonets? Or patent life vests in case of ship-wreck? Not surprisingly, Jane was 'constantly losing my keys my dear. All our things except what the two carpet bags will hold must go tomorrow so I shall be limited to snuff colours'.[149]

No doubt Jane had heard Martineau's advice, learned 'while beating about in the Mediterranean', which she outlined for the young Alfred Webb:

> I shd recommend a bath every morning. I see there are baths on deck in the Hempsyke. I used to have a bucket of sea water down, every morning; & carried a little tub; & it was a prodigious solace, I assure you.
>
> Of course, [Alfred] knows all about taking all manner of old linen, to throw overboard when dirty. Ireland has a fine reputation for old clothes; & it will be hard if she can't, like a good mother-country, supply her son with rags enough for a voyage. Slippers for deck, of course. Good shoes, you doubtless know, are awfully expensive out there. He must take a good stock. – Let him abstain from acid drinks at sea, in thirsty climates. Where fresh water is stinted, there is, for most folks, nothing like malt liquor. – Finally don't let him get alarmed at his appetite, when 300 miles out. If he finds he wants to eat a whole leg of mutton, let him be assured that others have felt so before him. – If he is likely to mind the <u>light</u> on board (always a trouble to me) let him eschew coloured spectacles, & get (from Dollond's) the wire-woven goggles that people wear in the desert. It might be wise to have them ready for Melbourne. They fit round the eyes, keeping out flies, & freely admit the air, while softening the light.[150]

People generally learned what to take from emigrants' handbooks, and from advice handed on from friends and relatives who had already made the voyage. One can imagine Tante Minne and Jeannette recalling sailing to and from Chile. David's brother John had already emigrated to Buffalo in New York State, and Jane's brother Louis and sister Louise had written about their respective journeys to Philadelphia and India. As Jane's long voyage was to be in the arduous conditions of a sailing ship, the packing of suitable equipment and clothing for the voyage itself was important. David's soon-to-be colleague, Pollock, had sent detailed instructions to his mother and sisters for their own voyage to Adelaide:

> Take no liquor with you as they are generally cheaper on board. You will find the moderate use of wine on board better than beer, and cheaper. Use crockery for your basins, jugs etc. Tin or metal becomes offensive, but for fear of breakages you should have duplicates. Have the basin deep, not shallow, for when the ship rolls the water is apt to fall out…Bring your own silver fork and spoon…As to dress – use your oldest things on sea. One bonnet will do you the passage. No-one thinks of your appearance…Keep all your dresses. You should get a new grey silk dress of some sort, and some cotton dresses…because of the hot weather. People here dress plainly, but well. Get drab silk bonnets – these hide the dust. You should also have a couple of black straws. Take calico, and make your underdresses at sea, as you will be right glad of work to do. Take a few well selected light books with you, as I don't think at sea one has much inclination for reading, because of the motion of the ship… Boots and shoes you can get here.[151]

Finding a ship was no easy process. The year before, at the height of the gold-rush, Dickens had given a sense of the 'struggling and elbowing' crowds at shipping offices:

> Legions of bankers, clerks, merchants' lads, embryo secretaries, and incipient cashiers, all going with the rush, and all possessing but faint and confused ideas of where they are going, or what they are going to do, beg of hard-hearted ship-brokers to grant them the favour of a berth in their last-advertised, teak-built, poop-decked, copper-bottomed, double-fastened, fast-sailing, surgeon-carrying emigrant ship.[152]

David was not able to book their passage on one of the new, elegant, swift and much-admired clippers (such as *Kangaroo* which was being loaded with the Cannans' iron house), nor on *Great Britain*, the only ship as yet to make the journey under steam. *Hempsyke* was of an earlier era, wide-bellied for carrying cargo rather than passengers, and typical of many ships on the Australia run. Now one of the White Horse Line fleet of Australian packets, the firm boldly advertised her as:

> A splendid, fast-sailing, British-built ship, loading in the East India docks. The provisions, fittings, and general arrangements (including baths and wash-houses on deck), will be of that superior description peculiar to this favourite and old-established line of packets, and a library of useful and entertaining books will be placed on board for the use of the passengers. She takes chief cabin and intermediate passengers only. Passage money 20 guineas and upwards. She carries an experienced surgeon.[153]

'Intermediate' meant a covered deck divided by bulkheads, temporarily fitted out with narrow tiered bunks along the sides with tables the length of the ship. Even the cabins, whether in the centre or stern of the ship, were cramped, so that intelligently fitting them out before departure mattered.[154] Jane cheerfully told Agnes after going to *Hempsyke* in the London docks on Wednesday 4th May that theirs:

> promises to be a wonderful size…Mamma and I and David and two Steel Yard young gentlemen all sat in it together quite comfortably – though I admit that I sat on the table, which is represented by my two square boxes one on the top of the other – There is a shelf all round or half round – I forget which – within a foot or so of the ceiling – with a ledge three inches high at the front – on which we can place almost all our possessions – the washhand stand is a scientific one – with a plug in the basin, to let the water

through into the pail at the bottom – Your chair has been fitted with cushions and is very comfortable indeed – We have more eatables and goodies that I think necessary – but we can give them away or live on them in Australia when provisions are dear.

On Monday we [packed] till 8 when we adjourned to Mrs Chadwick's. Mr C gave David a book about money and was very lively and talkative – at 10 we came home and packed again till after 11 and at 12 Mamma and Mary arrived and we talked till 1…David has never got the coat and hat yet – but at the worst he must turn out and get them at Plymouth for I won't let him go without them if I can help it.[155]

She told Mrs Cannan that the cabin, with space saved by a sliding door, and 'quite large enough to dance a hornpipe in', would look charming when the white counterpane was on the bed and a red tablecloth over the two boxes that made the table.[156] To Jeannette, on the eve of sailing, Jane wrote:

No W.C. in it as we partly thought – but never mind – I suppose we can do in Rome as the Romans do – there is a splendid shelf round two sides with a ledge in front – and a rod which takes up and down – where we can put everything, almost that we possess…a good many things go under the bed – which is the handiest little thing in the world – dividing itself in two – and lifting itself up at the ends.

[Yesterday the firm wished to make me] a present to the value of five pounds. We wanting nothing in the way of plate or clothing or jewellery…[David] knew we had no kitchen utensils – but did not like to ask for them – so said he would see – and Mamma has put him up to asking for a dinner service. [Mrs Rogers] told Mamma privately that she and Mr Rogers approved of Mr Cannan's choice – I mean of a wife – not of a dinner set…

<u>He</u> will be glad to get off – <u>she</u> rather shudders at the first seasickness.[157]

Jane and David, able to afford the cost of London lodgings, postponed their embarkation by joining the ship down the Thames at Gravesend. In *David Copperfield* Dickens captured the jumbled, crowded confusion that greeted boarding cabin passengers if they peered downwards, where 'every age and occupation seemed to be crammed into the narrow compass of the 'tween decks.'[158] On board *Hempsyke*, one hundred and thirty passengers, including twenty-six women and eighteen children, tried to create some order in their cabins or narrow berths. Jane and David watched a passenger seized for debt – and congratulated on his return. And then the fearful sailing into the open sea. From Plymouth Jane scribbled to Jeannette 'positively the last opportunity per pilot' while *Hempsyke* anchored briefly to take on more provisions and passengers. Having seen something of the naval fleet and bought a mug and basin from a waterborne trader,

> The anchor is up or getting up, there has been a muster of the steerage passengers and our cabin people are here – more than enough to sit at the table – Seven sheep have come on board [and] bundles of hay for them to eat…We are off and must go up to see the bay which is fine – so good bye for the present.[159]

FIVE

The floating home: *Hempsyke*

Alfred Webb and his cousin William Thompson, having travelled by steamer from Dublin, joined *Hempsyke* at Plymouth. Later in his life, Webb remembered that, as so often was the case for ships sailing out of London,

> She had heavy weather coming down [the English Channel] and did not arrive until the 14th. All was confusion on board, and my Father left us feeling we would have a bad time…
>
> The Hempsyke was an old style oak and teak built East Indiaman of 700 tons register with a poop deck, under which was the "cuddy" in which we first cabin passengers lived… There were some twelve of us in the first cabin besides the Captain and first mate, miserably lodged and fed…We were a mixed set, mostly young men, many of them wild – one especially so – a Mr Grote, nephew of the historian. Two married couples – a Mr Campbell and his giddy young wife, and Mr & Mrs Cannan. He was a clear sighted, somewhat sarcastic Scotchman; she what the Americans would call "a lovely woman." She evidently suffered much in the rough company and surroundings…
>
> No one who has not voyaged in [one] can have any conception of the amount of motion and tossing in a vessel of the Hempsyke class.[160]

Jane put a brave face on the company and conditions and instead described finding her sea legs and the gradual establishment of order:

The second Sunday was as rough as the first – and as sick – I began to think Sundays were particularly disagreeable – as on the third it rained – but last Sunday the 29th May was better and we had the agreeable change of hearing our doctor read prayers – We believe that he had been secretly thankful that the bad weather had saved him before. He was however ably supported by young Thompson whose "cheek" was of great service on this occasion – he read the responses and lessons and found the places for the poor doctor who knows no more about the order of reading the church service than the door post and was nervous accordingly.

We have an immense awning stretched partly over our particular deck and partly over the lower deck where the "intermediates", as they are always called, abide – The doctor had …a large cask swathed in flags for a desk. While the intermediates at least about three dozen of them – sat orderly on benches which had been hauled up from Pandemonium or "tween decks" the place where they sleep and dine etc… we sat up in our poop forming a kind of gallery – but could not hear – and David descended as I mean to next time.

You will say it is like me to describe the church first thing but it really was interesting enough and we enjoyed Sunday more than other days – because doing nothing was proper and the church into the bargain – the people were very nicely dressed – those that take pains at all – and Mrs Campbell and I were inspired to put on clean print dresses – It is also worthy of remark that we had three courses at dinner and some plum pudding was actually sent out as everybody had had enough!

Since Sunday it has been very hot and no one is very energetic and more of them sit below – We carry up Agnes' American chair and Ellie's hassock and establish ourselves

in a certain side of the deck – I work at my embroidery for
Agnes' and Maggie's habitskirts and it gets on fast though
I generally work in gloves with the tips cut off – David
reads in gasps [due to the ship's movement] and we have
occasionally conversations with our friends among whom
shine conspicuous the doctor – our fast friend.[161]

The doctor, Edwin Hall, probably working his passage as a means
of emigration, was singularly ill-equipped for the experience. He was
described by Webb as prone to hang 'in the rigging for our amusement,
[and to] give us a lecture, but was so foolish afterwards as to leave about
the book out of which he had copied it'.[162] Pollock had discovered
his ship's doctor to be an 'absolute goose', who was unmasked for
foolishly improbable tales of his life in the West Indies, and mocked
the more after he appeared at dinner under the influence of drink.[163]

As various schemes to assist emigrants developed, so the health
of the human cargo became a concern of both home and colonial
governments. Passenger Acts reduced the gross over-crowding and
consequent disease levels, and improved the food supplied. All ships
carrying more than fifty passengers had to have a surgeon (as did the
convict transports), whose authority was on a par with the captain's.
These doctors had a public health role, and were also expected to
take, as we have seen, the Sunday services, and to provide lectures
and educational events. Unfortunately, the merchant marine found
it difficult to attract and retain high calibre men, and an inclination
to alcohol featured in complaints.[164]

Hempsyke's small group of cabin passengers, to be thrown closely
together for who knew how many weeks, would have warily scanned
each other as they ate their first meals around the shared table in
the cuddy (or saloon). As the only other lady in that group, Mrs
Campbell was of particular interest to Jane. She had already written
from Plymouth to Jeannette that the Campbells were

evidently a bridal couple (how knowing I am becoming).
[She is] little and natty looking – though she had one

13 John Leech: 'The pound and the shilling': the hugely successful Great Exhibition of 1851 at the Crystal Palace had introduced an unsettling social mixing to London. The long voyage to Australia was also considered as preparation for more egalitarian ways. (Punch)

THE POUND AND THE SHILLING
'Whoever Thought of Meeting You Here?'

wristband pinned up with a pin, last night and this morning breakfasted with no undersleeves to a merino frock – She has a more coarse bonnet and blue veil – and a mantle & hood of thick duffle and looks very neat – outwardly...[165]

Mr Campbell...is going up to the diggings to keep some sort of merchandise there – and has a tent and an emigrants kitchen, and such like affairs – We cannot exactly understand what he means to do – but he calls himself a merchant and had a store once in California – David insists on his being an imposter.[166]

A certain Goldsmith[167] who has joined – looks like a regular gold digger with a sunburnt countenance as David says of him – The sooner he gets off to the diggings the better for he looks like nothing but quiet muscular strength and good tempered placidity – A certain John Groat[168] not yet explored – not interesting at present and rather gloomy – A certain Watson[169] – well got up with elaborate whiskers and good complexion with a brother just like him, and two sisters – who came to see him off – He has hardly spoken yet. [170]

The cabin passengers, then, included young men whose prospects of gentlemanly occupation in Britain were dim, tradesmen, and merchants or 'commercials' like David, attracted by the money and opportunities that gold had created in Victoria. Such was probably a typical cross-section of cabin passengers on the Australian runs at the time, mirroring the new, and sometimes rough, meritocracy that Australia was ushering in for its white settlers. While the great Atlantic steamers and the India-bound ships reflected – or even exaggerated – the traditional class system with the captain's table for the elite, the system was more hit-and-miss in the cuddies and saloons to Australia.[171] Pollock's fellow cabin passengers had included a woman going out to join relatives who were publicans, two educated young men who aimed to farm, another educated young man who had worked in a foundry and got mixed up with a young lady in Bath which resulted in having his passage paid but no idea of what he should do in Australia, and a lawyer and his family. Pollock, like David, had lost his father who had been a partner in a Dublin wholesale druggist firm, and seen the family's security erode as a result. Despite support from well-off uncles, Pollock's efforts to establish his own business in the same field failed. Hence his move to London in 1845 and employment as a correspondence clerk with Morewood & Rogers, a post which had already seen him travel to Geneva, France and Italy.[172] Pollock and David, then, shared a double migration – from Ireland or Scotland to England, and thence to Australia in the cotinuing search for enough money to maintain status.

★

Three and a half weeks into the voyage Jane had more detailed observations of her fellow cabin passengers:

[Mrs Campbell] is a pretty little thing – but nothing in her...Sometimes I pace the deck with her after tea while Mr Campbell smokes but they sit a good deal in their cabin and as I only attack her when she is alone we don't have too much of each other's company...It is wonderful to perceive how little patience David has...and how he hates to hear people talk ignorant nonsense!.. Mr Campbell however really does give himself airs and is very poor in his style of conversation – besides looking like a sort of third rate brigand, with his black hair and whiskers – scarlet sash around his waist &c &c...

Goldsmith, with the "digging" countenance amuses us by wearing a sort of ostling dress and working like a born ostler – it is a treat to see him blacking his shoes or sweeping his berth out or carrying his bedding up to air – he has an unusual genius, and on Sunday night he and a lot of them sang church music assisted by accordion and flageolet – He comes from Suffolk – and is always bringing forward his parish – or quoting what his father says – which amuses the more cosmopolitan passengers not a little. Watson is also musical and astronomical while the Baker[173] set, the four whom I mentioned as coming from one village – turn out to be drapers – There were two tall and two short ones – two lads whom I described as good tempered and merry. In the one I was not mistaken and he is as merry as ever but the other was so sick and ill that he wanted to be left at Madeira if we only could land him. His friends had been against his going and now he repented and would have given anything to get back – He is rather sullen now and often sunk in argument or at cards in a silly pig headed obstinate way...

The doctor is the greatest original we have – he is always in hot water when he has not fallen asleep – He is very excitable and comes out with everything that enters his head – generally without fear or favour – He holds that no one ever got rich without robbing their fellow creatures – that human nature is depraved and self-seeking – he also holds that he himself has been so wicked that he quite deserves to go to Hell – and sometimes has fears over being so long at sea – and wonders whether he should buy a few acres of land in Australia when he gets there. The Intermediates tear him to pieces and he alternately gets them up with his medical comforts – to wit ale and wine and such like…Between times he falls asleep and the steward from Pandemonium may expostulate as much as he likes – he still says he is coming and sleeps on especially if he happens to be in the American chair.[174]

Webb, meanwhile, was much liked by Jane and David for his modest, literary, and generous nature 'without any conceit or affectation', for his shabby clothes and higgledy-piggledy habits and for his intention to support himself by whatever work he might find and to see the world.[175] Jane wrote of his coming to

beg me to sew a button on his wristband during which process he holds out his hand like a child – and expects me to sew it on firm – at other times he gathers notes whether pickles are wholesome or says in the same tone I have had a feast on [Tennyson's] In Memoriam…He is only 19 but has been rather ground down with bad health I suppose – he is rather bigoted for Ireland but does persist readily in his opinion. [176]

Webb later recalled how he and Thompson 'spent many an hour in the mizzen top talking over old times and our future in Australia… the sails bellying out above and below us, the wide sea stretching away to the horizon around.' Webb helped the crew, and 'seldom felt more elated in my life than when first able to go aloft and set one of the royals by myself.' He later crewed on another sailing ship, so taken was he with the experience of 'the spray flying in over the weather bulwarks, the ship staggering and plunging.'[177]

Central to the saloon's life and to the safety and progress of the ship was, of course, the captain. Pollock had found his to be all he should be – firm in command, a good sailor and careful about the comfort of his passengers. He was lucky – attempts by the Board of Trade to upgrade training and the supervision of captains' conduct had resulted in little more than the setting of a low general standard. Significantly, masters and first officers had to submit not just proof of six years' experience but of 'habitual sobriety' if sailing south of the equator; not surprisingly passengers who could afford to do so travelled by shipping lines known for higher standards.[178]

Hempsyke's master, Captain Victor Toloubrof Howes, was described by David as having no manners and conceited enough for two. Jane judged him as fonder of the ship's cats than people, 'as treating us all rather as if he suffered us'[179], and

> a sort of brute to his fellow creatures – not apparently so much from malice or innate cruelty but from ignorance, narrow mindedness – and an insane belief that he must keep up his dignity.[180]

What an alarming realisation this must have been as the voyage got underway.

★

The voyage was a transition for Jane and David in that after their short spell of lodgings and packing, it encapsulated a period of marriage, away from relatives and concentrated in the private space of the cramped cabin. Jane, looking back on the voyage, laughingly described herself struggling to make the bed in rough weather when all the heavy bedding fell back on her. And

> I quite enjoyed sweeping up and putting everything straight in expectation of David's coming down to write or read –

or be on the bed, and of hearing him say our cabin was the nicest place on the whole ship – it really was…and our cocoa nut matting kept ours very nice…so we were quite furnished and very snug – after the heat was over when it was calm we enjoyed our little room very much and wondered what people required so much space for at home.[181]

The Cannans' berth was considered more comfortable and lighter than the Campbells' on the stern, which was darkened by the deadlights (shutters) in bad weather. So

we often have visitors in, we have three seats besides the whole bed…and we have had several select lunch parties to eat stewed biffins [dried apples] which the cook does for us, and we had a card party in last night, besides Mrs Campbell coming occasionally with her work and Mr Webb constantly appearing at the entrance, with his "Can I go in?" instead of "May I come in?" – I sometimes play chess with young Thompson in our den too – and sit there nearly always now as it is far more comfortable and warm than the cuddy and better lighted at night. Young Thompson is studying German and I give him what help I can.[182]

Everyone had time on their hands during the ninety three days' voyage. Cards was one gentlemen's amusement – whist and 'vingt un' – and draughts, and, as the weather improved, quoits on deck. Webb began editing and copying out a weekly, *The Mermaid*, with poetry, articles, and a 'really valuable portion of it is Mrs Cannan's little pen and ink sketches of incidents on board.' Jane explained that

Mr Ordish writes flowery descriptions of albatrosses & dolphins and things of that kind – Mr Miller writes doggerel generally humorous abuse of [fellow passengers], David writes miscellaneous articles – mock journals of passengers on the Hempsyke, riddles and definitions suited to the occurrences of the week – facetious bills of health signed by the doctor, and occasionally a grave article on the atmosphere which it is suspected no one reads but the editor. I occasionally furnish an illustration in pen and ink – It made a little variety but is certainly not first rate on the whole – and I hardly think it will last till we get to Melbourne.[183]

Gossiping about shipboard romances among the intermediates; looking out for evidence of southward movement in the stars, in porpoises, flying fish, sharks, and birds; running auctions, and betting on the day of arrival; making 'toffy' from the doctor's medical stores – these filled the hours for the cabin passengers. The long cuddy table was playfully divided into the House of Lords at the captain's end, and the House of Commons, presided over by Mr Plant the mate at the other (where the Cannans sat). As the journey wore on, Mr Campbell became more aloof and shut himself and his wife in their stern cabin, a Mr Pelly quarrelled with everyone, cheated at cards and disgusted others with his long finger nails. Mr Ordish, a mild man who shared the other stern cabin with him and two others, found himself punching Pelly after what everyone agreed was sustained provocation on Pelly's part.[184]

With no stops and generally out of sight of land, the greatest excitement was the sighting of other ships: Jane reported the sighting of 'the Mercia and [we] signalled a long conversation – She is also for Port Phillip – had left about the same time as ourselves and had also crossed the line on the ninth'.[185]

David, explaining to his mother that nothing but sea and sky might be seen for days on end, and that reading was difficult with the motion of the ship, became preoccupied with food:

Now for what we have to eat!!! To breakfast One Roll (hot) of bread – Rice and a vegetable – fried salt bacon, cold salt beef, and sometimes pork and sometimes mutton chops – also coffee falsely called – Lunch at 12 Biscuit Cheese and

Water – dinner Fresh Meat, meat pie, preserved meat, tripe, preserved potatoes and rice every day – Soup and cheese one day – and plum pudding or Rice pudding the other day. Tea biscuit and tea, very bad tea horrid – supper biscuit and water – The Ship biscuit not at all amiss.[186]

Jane too frequently mentions eating:

We enjoyed the preserves amazingly – David was the best hand at the strawberries and I beat him hollow at black currants. At one time strawberries were too sweet for my squeamishness…Mrs Doerings marmalade is a little fermented but quite eatable and it comes out at tea, and helps the biscuit and water – David and Webb impounded with the steward for bad tea in a morning instead of bad coffee – I stick to cold water and since they have given us rice to breakfast to eat like a vegetable with the salt meat I get on very well for it is very good with jam and bearable with brown sugar – Our fowls and ducks lasted till this week though we had four every day – and now we are devouring a pig – I have never had salt meat to dinner yet though I sometimes have <u>preserved</u> meat pie and those who want two helps of meat have always to finish with the salt junk or pork.[187]

David, perhaps passing on tips for others in the family who might follow him, instructed his mother that:

Everyone who goes to Australia ought to bring a [water] filter, plenty of preserves…also biscuits and arrowroot. Anything that requires cooking is a nuisance and no good whatever unless there are only a few passengers as the cook is worked like a horse. Gingerbread too is good – luckily we brought all the things named and only regret we had not brought more…

We have still three sheep and eight live pigs – The sheep are so so, the pork is for pork, excellent…We are allowed 6 pints of water daily for each individual, this includes both washing and cooking as well as drinking – The former is therefore only about two tumblers full and not over clean either. The water is pretty good on the whole, it always smells except when it stinks, but the latter is the exception and it is as good as I expected. Jane has been well enough always excepting for seasickness and I never was better in my life excepting that I am sick of the sea and squeamish in the mornings and when the weather is rough.[188]

The great marker of progress was crossing the Line. Despite the captain's discouragement, on July 9th Neptune, with a scalloped tin pot crown and a red herring on the prongs of a trident, emerged with his entourage. A money-box was jingled to which most passengers contributed rather than endure the shaving and ducking in a makeshift bath in a sail, though Webb and Thomson and other young men volunteered themselves as victims. After some horseplay, Jane watched the opportunity to right some wrongs:

the intermediate cook, a dirty little fellow, was ducked with gusto [and] a man who had publicly struck his wife and roused the indignation of the whole ship was often called for but wisely paid his fine and kept out of danger. They ended about 1 oclock with a universal skirmish with buckets of water during which finale the women and children came up on our deck for safety.[189]

Then came the great heat of the tropics. While the men could bathe and cool themselves on deck, Jane and Mrs Campbell were much more restricted. Jane compared notes with Jeannette's experience of sailing to and from Chile:

I was so hot myself that I could not do anything and quite hated my hands and feet, while my hair turned into hay and could not be smoothed at any price…I never "got the length" of being obliged to lie in a through draught in a state of semi nudity such as you described. Nevertheless the old thin garments which Tante Minne had put in were great comforts to me – I fancy you would have an awning in your ship and that would make a great difference – I did wear gloves when I could bear – but not always and escaped without sore hands though they were on the verge once – I never wore the gingham bonnet till today as it was too stuffy about the ears – and far hotter than the straw which is a fine specimen by this time, and not exactly the thing to land in as was intended…During the heat we had a wet day or two – had to keep below – that was horrible rain coming down with tremendous force in bucket fulls, and still the air not perceptibly cooler – The intermediates caught water in a sail hung up for the purpose and the popular costume was…bare legs and feet. We had a glut of water too, our can being quite full for once in its life…I drank vinegar with great relish during the hot weather and was even getting deluded into port wine & water, and I was as much disgusted as I should have been at home when one evening in the dark I inadvertently took a great gulp of David's brandy and water.[190]

Following the usual route, they sailed down the western Atlantic to pick up the strong westerlies in the far southern latitudes:

We passed a rocky uninhabited island called Trinidad, [the Baker boy] insisted to the captain that he was ready to land and take his chance – if the captain would put him ashore, there are goats and figs on the island which looks not unlike Arran at a distance, we had it in sight the whole day and a great treat it was, as through the glasses we could see the very rocks and stones, and the shadow of clouds on the splintered rocks were refreshing to behold – Cape hens and pigeons too began to appear & were pretty to watch, though it was vexing to see people shoot at them.[191]

Beneath the Cape of Good Hope, the passengers began hoping they might be in Melbourne in thirty days. The weather grew colder and rougher, but the Cannans' berth was snug. Despite the tremendous gales, sometimes with seas so high that the ship had to run before the wind with no sails at all, Jane declared that they never missed a meal,

> though it was rather snatching work to get the food into your mouth before it was thrown over your shoulder – It was wonderful how the steward and cook got through their work and it was wonderful to see how cheerfully the first mate, Mr Plant, would come down out of the storm to his meals, insisting that there must be some Jonah on board, or we could not have such a continuance of bad weather.[192]

The cabin passengers had the cuddy for mutual comfort during the rough weather when all were anxious, Jane writing

> We were hardly sea sick but felt seedy at times, besides feeling ill after bad nights caused by the rolling of the vessel and the disturbances and frights from the bumps, shocks and crashes, which accompanied the striking of great waves against the side of the vessel. She rolled over so frightfully at times (to my inexperienced ideas) that over and over again I thought she had lost her balance and could not right herself again, and that the next sound would be the water soaking everything in the cuddy…The doctor was however far worse than I and as he felt lonely, poor wretch he used to wander out of his solitary cabin at night, and prowl into the other more populous ones and make some of his fellow

passengers very angry by waking them…He often thought we were going down – and after a miserable night used to be intensely relieved when Charlie the cabin boy came at 6 to sweep the floor and prepare for breakfast, showing that the ship's company thought all right.[193]

★

What of the hundred or so intermediate passengers? Described by Webb as 'mostly low English', he thought there were 'very bad gettings on amongst some of the women'.[194] David quoted the Scottish ship's carpenter, with whom he fraternized, as saying that most had saved Her Majesty the expense of giving them a long voyage (that is to say, they were of the convict class).[195] On the other hand, the presence of family groups on board – such as the nine Cowsticks – would surely have met with the approval of Dickens, and the 'emigrants' friends' in the fashionable charities such as Mrs Chisholm. These were sponsoring and supporting female and family emigration to counter the moral degradation assumed to be associated with the disproportionately male population in Australia, now at risk of further corruption given the money that gold was releasing.[196] Jane observed

one or two women on board who have left their husbands behind – are gone to make money as teachers – not quarrelled – but agreed to separate on account of poverty – rather odd the women going out and the man stopping at home is not it?[197]

Given the financial pressures which so many were under, voyages were generally a distinct and important phase in the emigration process. Information and tips were swapped, and bonds made that supported arrivals and settlers, and, partly to this end, there began a degree of mixing between the cabin and intermediate passengers. The intermediates danced quadrilles, polkas, and schottisches on their deck, joined by some of the cabin passengers, but not, David hastened to say, himself. While the cabin ladies were usually (and tediously) imprisoned by expectations of decorum, looking down on to the poorer passengers from the poop deck, Jane was bolder.[198] The cabin passengers took advantage of emigrants who

> are always ready to oblige us in any way that they can…we have been able to return a little civility through the medium of our biscuits and other goodies…They also consult David, when they have anything on their minds – and several of them have told him their histories, and the causes of their going from home – I have also the privilege of lending them pins and teaching one or two to knit, while they will fetch and carry for me in the most amicable manner – We were amused by finding out that they took David for 37! also that he looked so ill during the first seasickness that he could not live over the voyage.[199]

Jane gave an agreeable picture of the children and their mothers:

> The children all look jolly enough – on Sunday [church service] they had a little form for themselves and sat very virtuously most of the time – They run about – play with dolls made of their shawls – talk cockney – and the little boys read sometimes and the little girls sometimes sew rags – The mothers are wonderful women and always go about tidy and cheerful cooking and washing and always having time to sit with the babies and talk to each other.[200]

Jane and David were aware that conditions down below were appalling and especially so in rough weather. The noises of heavy seas striking the ship, wind in rigging, the crew's commands, distressed animals, and voices through thin partitions, together with the inevitable smells and general seepage of the ship, were magnified in these quarters.[201] Jane was horrified by

> the water coming into the hatchways even though they

were closed – The jumbling of such a crowd together at such a time must have been dreadful – Some of the women came up on deck yesterday and the day before, and we had some chat with them. One old Scotch lady was going out to her husband, and had had a dismal time – He was master of a vessel in the south sea trade – and when she had been to sea before it had been with him and she was very differently looked after – Poor thing it made me shiver when she described how she had sat in her berth shivering with cold and wet, for the water had come right into her bed – Another young woman – the one who got beaten by the husband at the outset – recounted how she had ruined all her clothes with putting them away under the bed – where water came in and rotted them before she was aware.[202]

The crew too suffered; bad as things were for the emigrants, in common with other merchant ships, their accommodation, diet and working conditions were worse. Webb remembered that:

Two of the crew died on the passage, as their mates said – at least in the case of one of them – from hard work, poor food, and neglect on the part of the Doctor…I see one of [their funerals] as I write – the vessel under shortened sail the spray and waves flying over the deck, the captain with difficulty keeping his feet as he hurriedly read a few words from the prayer book, the body sewn up in canvas plunging into the waves that came up on deck to meet it.[203]

The usual end-of-voyage expression of gratitude from passengers became problematic, the captain, according to David, deserving the intermediates' anger 'only too richly.'[204] David and Jane were appalled at the neglect of the sick sailors and the disrespectful burial. The testimonial, Jane wrote, 'only got 8 supporters out of fourteen – the intermediates would not sign because of the word <u>kindness</u> being introduced.'[205]

As they neared the Australian coast, future plans became the great, cheering, and perhaps, worrying topic of conversation. The crew, gold diggings in mind, were

> getting saucy as they near land, and it is supposed all will bolt, who can get the chance – the carpenter, who is a very superior sort of man, means to go and Plant the first mate has a quarrel with the captain, and would fain to go too.[206]

The doctor, Jane continued, realising that life for a single man, most likely in a tent, would be difficult, consulted the steward and passengers over the possibility of a wife. He inquired into 'the sewing capabilities of a certain Miss Anderson an elderly substantial lady

14 *Jane Cannan: 'Collegiate Institution [St Peter's], Adelaide', built in 1849. It and the Bishop's Palace were roofed in Morewood & Rogers' galvanised corrugated iron. Both buildings were based on designs from England, probably by Henry Stuckey (Lewis, 2010, provides the architectural detail and original locations for this and subsequent pictures). The initial plan was for David and Jane to join the business in Adelaide, at that time a more established city than Melbourne.*
(Royal Historical Society of Victoria)

among the intermediates who would as soon marry the doctor as I would.'[207]

Thompson was unsure of his position as his father was a struggling carpenter with eight children, and Webb was still determined not to go home for two or three years. The Cannans, Jane said, were

…rather given to speculating what we shall do on our arrival, and to considering where we are to settle at first… We have in imagination cooked lots of dinners, established uncle Charles' desk in an ornamental position, and hung the Pritts' pictures – lined the iron house with calico – and had a whist party in the parlour, surrounded the house with a blooming garden and fushia [sic] hedges – and sat outside the front door on the American chair and the hassock.[208]

At last, on 15th August, ninety-three days after leaving Plymouth, they reached Hobson's Bay, and were close to land. Next day, the passengers were delivered by steamer to the wharf in Sandridge. Jane and David walked the couple of miles up to Melbourne, carrying their carpet-bag and travelling writing desk.[209]

Domain Road.

15 *Jane Cannan: 'Domain Road', Melbourne. A large single-storey verandahed house stands on the left with distant views of the city and a road gang in the foreground. Perhaps gentlemen who had no skills to fall back on were among their numbers, a phenomenon observed with amusement by working class immigrants. (National Library of Australia)*

Six

Totally unfit for genteel people: Melbourne

> 'The equality system here would stun even a Yankee.'[210]

Each Victorian era, argued the historian Asa Briggs, had its shock city, from which erupted novel, alarming and exhilarating ways of life and values.[211] For the 1840s he named Manchester, for the 1850s Melbourne takes centre-stage.[212]

Here the first shock for newcomers was the realisation that their carefully saved pounds could buy only a fraction of what they had bought in Britain or Ireland. Webb was far from alone in finding his small investment worthless:

> When I was leaving home extraordinarily high prices were reported in Melbourne for all articles of clothing. Uncle James Webb confided to…my care a considerable consignment for sale…On our arrival we found the market utterly glutted from all parts of the world, and we had to dispose of the goods at prices far below those they would have brought at home, not to speak of the cost of carriage…I brooded much on it morbidly, and persuaded myself that I was the cause of the loss and that perhaps I could never return…

I often witnessed pathetic scenes upon the wharves – helpless families of immigrants landed and not knowing where to turn – a young man far gone in consumption brought on shore in a chair. I pitied greatly a delicate half starved looking French lad trying to sell lemonade.[213]

As a consequence of the gold discoveries Melbourne had become the most expensive city in the world. Land values ballooned, partly because the money from gold had few outlets in which to be invested. Moreover, vast quantities of merchandise continued to arrive from Britain and the USA, destabilising markets. In 1853, a hundred and thirty four ships reached Melbourne from the United States alone, bringing one and a half million pounds worth of goods. An American merchant wrote of the reckless speculation, the bay 'nothing but one complete forest of masts...between six and seven hundred [ships] were crowding each other for more room'.[214]

For the adaptable there was easily available work, with huge demand for labour in quarries, mills, breweries and tanneries. Webb became a wharf-clerk with Beaver and Stevens at £4 a week. Goods were unloaded from vessels in Hobson's Bay and brought ashore in lighters. Webb's job was to have these goods carted up to the stores, past the ubiquitous bullock teams bringing down wool for export or taking goods up to the diggings.

What Webb quickly noted in his lowly, crowded boarding house was a second shock: the 'strange collection of young men of all classes from home'. Among those chasing jobs were gentlemen – the poor but enterprising younger sons, those educated for over-crowded professions who were unwilling to risk social declassification at home, and those who sought escape and adventure. Some – feckless Micawbers hoping something would turn up, and wild young men – had been pushed out by families disembarrassing themselves in what historian Thomas Keneally terms above-decks transportation.[215] A case in point was Pollock's brother Alexander, 'a pretty far advanced scamp', who had been encouraged to join relatives in the new colony for a new start, in Alexander's case as a commission and land agent.[216]

Jane too noticed these strange consequences of the great gold-induced tumult, citing their ship's doctor following, dog-like, the man who had waited on him on the ship.[217] She described how gentlemen were quickly reduced to selling their clothes, and told Mary Cannan:

> how overstocked the place is with young men who want vague situations, and have learned no trade before they came – Our landlady knows several young men, the sons of gentlemen at home, who are working on the roads here [which] require a good deal of attention to keep them in temporary order, and any one may earn 10/- a day – it is not hard work – but uninteresting and somewhat ignominious.[218]

Pollock had witnessed the extraordinary social revolution in the gold fields where 'working like galley slaves, are Miners, Bushmen, gardeners, bullock drivers, Masons, Doctors, Tailors, Architects, "gentlemen at large" (returned convicts) and Parsons.' Like others, he asserted (perhaps with his fingers crossed) to those at home that anyone could 'get on' who was willing to work hard, much to Australia's benefit.[219]

By 1853 the gold fields had sucked tens of thousands of men out of half-developed Melbourne. Characteristically Jane noticed the impact on children:

> I saw an advertisement this morning "Wanted a boy or girl of 12 years of age to cook for three men living in a tent near Melbourne". What do you think of a boy cook of 12 years old![220]

She remarked that children were very precocious:

> You will see little imps of boys keeping shops in the master's absence and going about with horses that look like elephants to them, a little girl is consulted by her mother what should be had for dinner, or how she should step out a polka, and

a little boy from the country is said to have cut his father in the streets of the town when he was sent to school there.[221]

Moreover, she had heard of women, their husbands at the diggings, having to apply for government rations.[222] There was novelty and even amusement in uninhibited shamelessness, Jane reporting:

> There are some curious laws here – a man is fined 40/– for being drunk, but he pays it quite willingly and pleads guilty, saying he <u>was indeed glorious drunk</u>! A woman is fined for the same offence several times, and is at last put in prison for a time because the mag. is <u>tired</u> of seeing her.[223]

Fortunes were being made and lost, and caution, respectability and honesty mocked. Was Melbourne a Mammon's domain of greed, of despoliation of the earth's riches, and of drunkenness (with over one hundred pubs or hotels) from which the genteel should flee?[224] Or was it also 'truly a wonderful place, a perfect Babel wherein men of all nations talk and sing and fight and embrace'?[225] Pollock had been honest enough to qualify his deploring of the 'intense desire to be rich, the speculation, the hardness, the selfishness so apparent throughout the community' that he had already encountered in Adelaide by admitting that he too wanted a little more cash, but 'not for the mere sake of getting rich – I would very much like to be able to fulfill the injunction, and 'owe no man anything'.[226] Given his own insecurity, Pollock was mindful of those who struggled, for he was among the subscribers to Melbourne's Institution of Houseless Immigrants.[227] What played on his mind and drove the need for money was his heavy debt to Morewood & Rogers of £400, partly for his family's fares to Adelaide, with further debts to his godfather and uncle of £350 – amounts he optimistically hoped to clear in three to four years.[228]

★

Jane and David were fortunate in being received by Pollock, whom they found 'a very decent fellow' and lively, agreeable company, with courtly manners and musical talents.[229] At twenty-eight, close in age to David, and with three years' experience in the Australian colonies, he provided an invaluable introduction to the markets and way of life of southern Australia. Pollock had learnt to deal with the rough and tumble of managing employees. On his arrival in Adelaide he had found the Morewood & Rogers business in a state of disarray under a negligent, drunken manager, Mr Gell, and feuding staff. One of his clerks, a man Pollock had known in London, was sentenced to nine months imprisonment for embezzlement despite Pollock's plea for leniency on the grounds of the man's good character.[230]

Pollock's widowed mother and his sisters Isabella and Nannie had joined him in 1852. Business was good if not spectacular and he rented a comfortable Morewood & Rogers house in pleasant Norwood. Morewood & Rogers' store on Leigh Street, had a tremendous signboard, 'painted on it the Cabbalistic Words "Galvanized Tinned Iron".[231] The firm had already roofed Schneider's copper smelting plant at the extensive Burra mines in remote country north of Adelaide. Looking for other big commissions, Pollock secured an order to roof the Collegiate Institution of St Peters. The builder and Pollock's friend Edmund Wright supervised the construction using a Henry Stuckey design, as Jane was later to illustrate (see picture no 14).[232] She also drew the Adelaide Bishop's Palace, constructed by the same team, and similarly roofed. Pollock had written to Morewood & Rogers that 'As soon as the corrugated arrives we can do much business, as at present it is rather awkward to have nothing to show or offer but Tiles.'[233]

Pollock's responsibilities extended beyond ordering and selling roofing materials. Morewood & Rogers were interested in a return wool trade, placing difficult negotiations on a young man's shoulders, and later he was to send a shipment of gold to the firm. Pollock also suggested commodities to import of which he had more experience – pharmaceutical drugs, and Guinness, his godfather having family ties with the business.[234]

Continuation of the view from Mr Pollock's window

16 *Jane Cannan: 'Continuation of the view from Mr Pollock's window'. Half of a panorama drawn from David Cannan's colleague's house at 97 Little Lonsdale Street East (Moore, 2012). This house had doubled as Morewood & Rogers' original Melbourne office. Jane's precise eye for the burgeoning buildings and businesses of Melbourne is complemented by another foreground of simple domesticity; with goats, a mother and children, a washing-line, and waiting carts. (Royal Historical Society of Victoria)*

Later in 1852 Pollock moved to Melbourne. He worked hard to persuade the firm that Silas Harding, a successful Geelong merchant already trading in their products in the area, should be a partner, but Morewood & Rogers appear not to have followed this up. Pollock was soon advertising in the *Argus*

MOREWOOD, ROGERS & CO: Patentees of Galvanised Tinned Iron. Temporary Office, Little Lonsdale Street East, a few doors from Russell Street. ANDREW JAMES POLLOCK, sole agent.[235]

It is likely that 97 Little Lonsdale Street East, a two-storey house of four rooms and a kitchen, was the Pollock family home; by the time the Cannans arrived, the firm's offices had moved to Flinders Lane.[236]

★

Finding money more interesting than his first sight of the Southern Cross, David naturally found Melbourne's booming prices and rents invigorating. He wrote to his brother James a few days after their arrival to say that they were well-lodged, and that

Our business is very brisk and we have no stock and our only complaint is that we have too little stuff sent out from London – Altogether I am very well satisfied with the place as far as business is considered. Land is ridiculously dear and all houses are not only dear in themselves but the immense cost of land makes them doubly so…The house we live in has five rooms and a passage and lets at about £365 per annum and is in Collingwood too where rents are lower than in Melbourne.

Jane has been making sketches of various things but I have none for you yet as she has been doing one or two of M & R's property which I want to send them and I have five already and very useful to them they will be…26 Flinders Lane is the office address if you wish to give it to anyone coming out – Carpenters, painters, tinmen and such like trades earn at present 30/- per day – labourers 10/- to 12/-, a working man pays for Board and Lodging and not at all comfortable either 30/- per week – Altogether it is a splendid country for a working man if he has £20 or £30 to land with and if he will put up with discomfort both on the voyage and on his arrival especially the latter…

I send you a newspaper in which you will see a note of thanks to A.J. Pollock of the new church of Galvanized Iron created at Prahran for the Wesleyans. I intend putting up a house in the neighbourhood, [much nicer] than any place near Manchester.[237]

The Wesleyan chapel was a cautionary tale: it became known as 'the Iron Pot': so hot could it become that a scheme to import further iron chapels was abandoned.[238]

★

If Melbourne was a rowdy, topsy-turvy bear pit, how did Jane experience it? Pitched into a world where ladies had to contribute to the physical work of running a house and producing food, had to walk because carts and carriages on rutted and often muddy roads were as unstable as a ship in a storm, and where familiar, intricate codes of deference and manners had been thrown into the air like packs of cards, she gives no sense of being daunted. Rather her letters are full of willingness to give Melbourne society a chance, and to roll her own sleeves up.

David being busy at Morewood & Rogers, it fell to Jane to collect the baggage from *Hempsyke*:

Mr Webb being my escort, it made a very nice day's pleasure trip for we went down the Yarra in a steamer and saw the approach to the town which we saw nothing of before – The Yarra winds so that it is 7 or 8 miles to Williamstown at the mouth of which the cut that we walked up from Liardet's

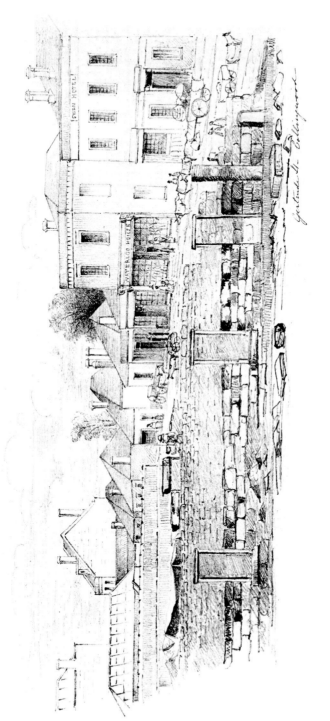

17 *Jane Cannan: 'Gertrude Street Collingwood' (Fitzroy). The Cannans lodged in this area when they arrived in Melbourne in 1853. The Swan and Waterloo Hotels are visible; the foreground is probably Napier Street and the building under construction the Leviathan Hotel. (Royal Historical Society of Victoria)*

beach was not more than two miles – At Williamstown we took a row boat to go to the Hempsyke which lay several miles out in the bay beyond the other ships, as the weather was beautiful, the row was very pleasant, and our gentlemanly boatmen rowed very well – The sailors had not then deserted the ship and looked quite pleased to see us again, Webb was very popular among them and indeed with all classes on the ship…

It was a beautiful day for seeing the bay and I was delighted with the winding river, the banks of which after you leave the town, are wooded with a sort of shrubby tree.[239]

Although Jane and David had no firm intention of settling, they had been ambivalent enough to have proposed to Mary Cannan that she join them once she had finished her work in Rome. Accordingly, Jane looked into teaching possibilities in Melbourne, but was discouraged. The English emigration charities were contributing to a surplus of governesses, artificial flower makers and ladies' companions in the colony, and the demand for teachers was low.[240] Jane told Mary she had heard of respectable women having no choice but to be a governess in the bush

where the people were so rough and the children so brutalised that young, well educated ladies were miserable… If you did come here I should fancy you would do better as an artist than as a teacher. People would like to have their portraits painted long before they would care to have their children taught drawing, and your German, Italian and Latin would all be wasted unless you were connected with the expensive schools.[241]

Added to which, Jane feared Mary would miss European art and literature, for the general shortage of books was causing David some frustration – tattered copies of *Sketches by Boz*, the *Waverley* novels of

Walter Scott, *Blackwood's Magazine* and old *Scottish Guardians* were lent around the lodgings – though the *Argus* occupied David's breakfasts satisfactorily.

Jane wrote to Jeannette, now Madame du Bois Raymond and living in bourgeois comfort in Berlin, that for ladies

> Melbourne is the very opposite in every respect to Valparaiso, and that therefore you need only just reverse everything to have a true picture…for here are the extreme of small houses & poor accommodation & with regard to the ladies being so waited on and kept in glass cases in Valparaiso…all ladies here must put their hand to, to "grease" the domestic wheel if not absolutely to turn it![242]

Jane had other models that prepared her for a more rugged life. Her sister Louise was suffering the heat, dust, disease and formidable travel arrangements of the Indian Army before the railway era. And in the USA, Louis had been living rough in forests, had survived cholera and dysentery outbreaks, endured heat and bitter winter cold, and travelled widely by horse.[243]

Nor was the Australian lack of deference wholly unexpected. In England's northern industrial cities such as Manchester a confident and growing working-class provoked anxiety about social stability. In an illustrative vignette in *North and South*, Mrs Gaskell describes her heroine, Margaret, colliding with the egress of mill workers:

> They came rushing along, with bold, fearless faces, and loud laughs and jests, particularly aimed at all those who appeared to be above them in rank or station. The tones of their unrestrained voices, and their carelessness of all common rules of street politeness, frightened Margaret a little at first. The girls, with their rough, but not unfriendly freedom, would comment on her dress, even touch her shawl or gown to ascertain the exact material…She

alternately dreaded and fired up against the workmen, who commented not on her dress, but on her looks, in the same open, fearless manner. She, who had hitherto felt that even the most refined remark on her personal appearance was an impertinence, had to endure undisguised admiration from these out-spoken men.[244]

★

In response to the desperate housing shortages that had greeted arrivals in 1852, feverish building work in Melbourne had produced over a thousand new buildings, many of stone, together with five large immigrants' reception centres. In the eastern suburbs, thousands of small houses had been quickly thrown together, often from whatever material was to hand. Melbourne's novel grid street plan in its centre had been laid out only fifteen years earlier, as it grew with the wool-trade.[245] Visiting in 1851, Pollock had noted that it was already a 'smart, stirring little town with a business-like appearance'.[246] It was a pretty place, he wrote, with fine shops, and 'the width of the streets & general plan of the place is so good that it has quite an important look…The people dress exceedingly well, quite tastefully in the extremity of the English "mode"'.[247]

While waiting for their iron house to arrive, and living in lodgings with a Mr and Mrs Kerr in Collingwood, Jane walked about town, remarking on the working men's blue and scarlet flannel shirts, the gaily dressed 'vulgar' women with 'groves of artificial flowers' on their bonnets, the great bullock teams lumbering along with their drays, and the tranquillity of the government paddocks. Undaunted by her straw-like hair flying out to the extent that Mrs Pollock threatened macassar oil and curls, Jane told Mary

> I often go down to the office in the afternoon and fetch away 'my husband' who goes with me to sketch and sits most by most patiently – I am trying to fill a little book with views of the town and buildings connected with galvanised

iron to send to Morewood & Rogers and I feel quite proud of doing anything which may be useful in business.[248]

Describing her routine in the lodgings,

> At one o'clock I fork out some lunch from the mysterious corner, which is a sort of amateur pantry, and after that go out generally with the sketch book, sometimes down to the office to fetch away David to go with me – Sometimes I go to the town for some trifle, and then roam through the streets looking at the shops & the people, sometimes I call at the Pollocks…I am going to buy an autographic press – by means of which I can print off pen and ink sketches – if I succeed in that it will be capital – but I am doubtful at present, as I am quite unused to printer's ink & ink-slabs, and talc powder and emery paper – I delighted Mr Kerr's heart by making him a view from his window – He is quite sure I could make my fortune rapidly by taking views, and is not half satisfied with me when I say I will try it when galvanised iron fails.[249]

She described to her brother-in-law James the wild-flowers, the beautiful spring gardens, the comfortable wooden gentlemen's houses widely spaced to avoid fire-risk, and a prettily situated house on the Yarra. Yet Jane knew that Melbourne was 'elbowing its way out' and cutting down trees[250], and was astonished by the:

> Camp like suburbs with their tiny houses, and…many thousands of people are accommodated in them…Canvass [sic] town is a village of tents, I counted roughly 200 ranged in streets, these lie at the foot of a grassy mound south of the town. Across the river at a little distance from the village stands a spare tent with <u>National School</u> painted on it in great letters.
>
> I want very much to go through canvass town and

our landlady has promised to take me, as she has some acquaintances there. I have been in one tent, belonging to a working man, connected with the galvanised iron, it was just large enough to turn in and not that when he and his wife and child were all in together. However, people who come out of ships, where they have lived three or four months do not feel that such a hardship, and it saves time and fatigue if you can reach all your worldly possessions without moving from your seat. This man's wife hospitably invited us in, on sunday afternoon, and gave us a very decent cup of tea each besides brandy and water – David sat on the bed, and I sat on the camp stool, while the woman took a bit of board – and sat between us and the doorway on the floor. The little fireplace was beside the door & had a chimney piece and pictures and ornaments – the chimney outside the tent was made of galvanised iron...These people are to move into a nice iron cottage of one good room, but instead of being delighted the woman said she had got so used to these things that she "hardly noticed"...They did all [the washing] outside, indeed a good table and several barrels always stand outside.

The wooden houses are made to look very neat occasionally and got up in imitation of stone – but there are also very rubbishy little sheds put together, and some houses are built of several materials – plenty of galvanised iron roofing, also a wooden roofing composed of small pieces, smaller than ordinary slate, called here shingle – I have also seen cottages like biscuit boxes made of sheets of tin and canvass roofs and galvanised iron doors. There is some capital blue stone here the geology of which we have not yet discovered, many buildings are composed partly of that and partly of brick...

The streets look very businesslike, and everyone seems to be about business but it is curious to see such wide streets with such low shabby buildings at the sides, and in many of them the mud is awful, after the least rain the gutters or ditches are so wide and deep I have to look out for a favourable place to cross, and in our common here there are ravines that it is impossible for me to jump over. On Sunday we had to go a good way to avoid one, and saw a few sheeps' heads, and other trifles of that kind lying at the bottom – they have no use for the heads of the cattle here – and at the slaughter houses on the banks of the river below the town we saw piles of oxen's heads which had been burnt and looked at first like firewood or something of that nature. Near a butcher's shop too we saw the sheeps' heads thrown away, and wished them in Great Britain where they would soon be carried off.

...The gentlemen here wear great top boots which they draw over their trowsers – fancy David in those striding over chasms or wading through mud in the winter – and in the summer fancy him wearing a white hat with a green veil to keep the dust out of his eyes. I am not so sure of this last though – for they say only newcomers do it & soon leave it off – As for me, if I don't wear Bloomer now – I never shall – Melbourne is the very place for that dress, but I shall get on famously with a pair of Westmoreland clogs, and I hope we shall soon see the streets mended, it is an exaggeration to say that the mud is knee deep sometimes but we have come just when the worst is over, we have had showers but only one wet day since we came, the mud is clayey and sticky, so it soon gets wet, and soon dries again.

The fires are all of wood here, and the fireplaces, brick hearths, with two low hobs of bricks, and the logs are laid across – we like them very much and were delighted to see a fire, after being without so long in the ship – There will be fires for three weeks yet, as the mornings and evenings are still quite frosty feeling though it gets hot in the day – we hear such various accounts of the heat and the climate that all we can do is to wait and judge for ourselves – so far we have found it very pleasant, windy certainly but not unlike a cold day in May in England…We walked six or seven miles on Sunday – and enjoyed ourselves very much, though Miss Pollock said it was a horrid day with a hot wind & that no old settler would have thought of such a thing – [251]

★

The disproportionately male population instilled caution with tales of robberies, murders and drunkenness. While Jane declared that they had great fun when they visited the Pollocks, listening to Andrew's funny anecdotes and looking through copies of *Punch*, they had an early tea as

In winter no one likes to be out after dark – the road is so full of holes that you may easily break your leg if you are not knocked down and robbed – stick up is the term for robbing here as it has been the custom for these wretches to tie their victims up to trees or fences.[252]

Nevertheless, Jane thought that a respectable community was forming, and believed

that we shall feel differently with regard to Melbourne, to what the older residents do, they have seen dreadful times, both of the riot and coarseness of the prosperous diggers… and of the distress of respectable people coming out, when there were literally no houses for them…Coming at a time of comparative improvement, I feel rather interested in the half finished state of things, and shall like to see it getting into order.[253]

1853 saw the start of desperately needed public works on roads, lighting, wharf construction and drainage. The dreadful state of local sanitation alarmed Jane, who saw 'the causes for epidemics & mortality, in the undrained state of the town, the absence of water supply, and

View in Richmond

18 Jane Cannan: 'View in Richmond'. A peaceful, domestic scene, with little houses dotted among trees; the two linked iron-roofed buildings in the centre, perhaps stores or workshops, were presumably Morewood & Rogers products. This may have been the basis of a sketch of Morewood & Rogers' buildings to send back to them.
(Royal Historical Society of Victoria)

the miserable dwellings'.[254] On such matters they would have been well informed by their fellow lodger, Mr Gale, an engineer at the new water works.[255] Melbourne's lack of clean water and the collection of stinking sewage in huge open gutters meant that, despite its wide and airy streets, the mortality rate during that period was actually worse than London's, and it was worse in some of the suburbs than the centre.[256] David thundered:

> Mr Chadwick could not find fault with the <u>way</u> anything is done, because there is not anything done. Water is got in carts from the Yarra at a cost of ¾d per gallon, the said Yarra having the pumps just below where the horses are washed & numerous woolwashing establishments being higher up the said river.[257]

19 Jane Cannan: 'View of suburban Melbourne'; the church on the left has an adjoining corrugated iron building, perhaps also drawn for the firm. (National Library of Australia)

The precariousness of life was evident. Pollock's sister Isabelle had lost her fiancé, a Mr Lefebvre, who had been Morewood & Rogers' reliable second-in-command in Adelaide. Pollock's other sister, Nannie, had married James McCrae, the doctor of the ship they came out in, and now a Justice of the Peace (a magistrate) at the diggings. However, Nannie 'has not very good health and is coming down to Melbourne shortly for her confinement.'[258] And the scamp of a brother, Alexander Pollock, had recently died of apoplexy, leaving a widow and small son.[259]

Jane's letters tell of other sad losses and she reminded herself that

> Melbourne is not a place to get worldly-minded in because you are constantly reminded of the shortness of life by the way people talk, and I mean to be very philosophical even if I cannot make my house into my little perfection that I imagined it…I can see very plainly that the little I want does not consist in antimacassars – nice clean table cloths, tidy drawers – a place for everything and everything in its place – but in something very different which I cannot elaborate because that wretch David will want to read the letter when he comes home.[260]

Unable to resist a sense of foreboding, Jane sent some of her hair to Jeannette to be made into a chain for David should she die.[261]

★

The couple of months spent in lodgings in Collingwood were happy ones. While David and Pollock went to Adelaide (which David much admired), Jane helped the landlady, drew, and visited Mrs Pollock, helping with her quilt-making for a Madagascar mission. She remarked to Jeannette that her seven months of marriage without a home were rather like a grand bridal tour, often in amusing company:

> We have been rather roused up by the McCraes coming down from the diggings and exciting us to all sorts of unwonted gaieties – Dr McCrae is very funny & kept us all laughing with his puns and nonsense…The three gentlemen, David, Mr Pollock and the Dr, had business at Geelong forty miles off – in the bay – and as both Miss P and I wished for the trip we went with them – I enjoyed it amazingly, though I was sick on the way there, and utterly wretched and miserable for two hours. We went by steamer one day

and came back the next – sleeping at an hotel & walking about the town and paying visits to people that they knew there. It is a large scattered town increasing rapidly, but not as bustling as Melbourne by a long way – its position in the bay is good and there is a pier for landing at once from the steamer, in two years there will be a railway between the two towns – and then I shall want to go again.[262]

Mrs Pollock she was beginning to find 'a bit of a fidget', a mother who had her son under her thumb, and was prone to give Jane unneeded opinions:

> Mrs Pollock often discourses to me of the hideous suspicion she entertains about some one being older than their husband! But I look very sympathetic & say nothing – they know David's age I believe – but not mine till I chose to tell!
>
> She is very kind in her way – she always sends me home with some trifle from scented soap to a pincushion with bows at the corners...She is very severe on useless wives though she has a notion that we ought to "arrange" our husbands – as Mrs Doering would say...I betrayed her into acknowledging that she had misgivings about what sort of person M & R would send out – as they had not distinguished themselves in sending out satisfactory underchappies. She said she had been very anxious but "Mr Canning" as she persists in calling him [but he] grows on her.[263]

Things were to change, however. Mrs Pollock decided to return to England accompanied by Andrew who 'is rather tired of the colonies, and having made some money now he can afford to go and his health will be better of the change'.[264] Between the lines one sees Mrs Pollock not wishing to stay with her two married daughters (Isabella had recently married William Hier, a Melbourne merchant). David would step into Pollock's shoes in Melbourne, paying two visits a year to Adelaide, and business being first rate, thought he might continue 'for a while if not always'.[265] He expected that communication with Morewood & Rogers in London would become easier and of course swifter with the introduction of the two-month overland mail service via Egypt.[266]

SEVEN

The iron house

It is gratifying to turn from the contemplation of [new arrivals']
hardships and discomforts to the invention of portable zinc houses
[which] from the nature of the material, and from the simplicity of
erection and removal, is well adapted to that object, and is already
in great demand. The emigrant who designs to enter upon business
may select one capable of forming an elegant showroom or store, with
a dwellinghouse attached...The external design is neat, though,
when ornaments are placed upon the roof, its claims to taste and
elegance will be more apparent. ('Portable Metallic Houses for
Australia', *The Times*, 1 April 1853)

Galvanised tinned iron, Plumbic Zinc, Patent tin plate, Galvanised
Iron welded tubing, Pump fittings, Rain water pipe, gutter ridging,
Brackets, wire, nails &c.
MOREWOOD, ROGERS & Co, Patentees.
D.A. CANNAN, Agent, 26 Flinders Lane east.
(*Argus*, 23 February 1854)

On his return from Adelaide, David hoped to

> set about erecting our house on our "landed estate" of ¼
> acre – [Prahran] is a very pretty neighbourhood and I think
> I shall like it well – Pollock returns to England in January
> next and I hope he and Morewood & Rogers will make it
> alright as his presence in London could be advantageous to
> me out here – If the times continue moderately prosperous
> I can make a large income but the expenses are tremendous
> – however I will do much better than in England.[267]

With David now satisfactorily installed in the galvanised iron
business, Jane admitted that she was not having to endure any
'roughing':

> I am not half colonised – & shall not be able to boast of
> all I did in Australia, with the exception of a little amateur
> carpentering & wood cutting I have done no more than
> what any country lady with a small house-hold would do.[268]

The housing of choice for those able to distance themselves from
the crowded tenements and terraces of 'home', was the thriving
low-density suburbia to Melbourne's east: Fitzroy, Richmond and
Collingwood, Prahran being just to the south of Richmond.[269]
The Cannans' new life in Melbourne – as for so many 'respectable'
immigrants – was a curious mix of the pioneering and the tamely
suburban. Paradoxically, suburbia was itself a pioneering form of
community, a life-style not yet in existence in Europe. The new
English suburbs were not spread out, but were concentrations of
comfortable houses in the more salubrious quarters of towns and
cities, upwind of the stench of industry, slums, and still inadequate
sanitation.[270]

The Cannans' plot on Gardiner's Creek Road (later Toorak Road),
was then very open:

I am quite delighted with the idea of being in such a rural situation, for though out of the town, it is not lonely as Prahran is a large scattered suburb – a <u>township</u> I believe they call it, with ten or twelve thousand inhabitants, though [they] are very invisible.[271]

To Jeannette, Jane described the novelty of Prahran as a 'village scattered for miles round without any visible nucleus but containing bakers and butchers shops, general stores, public houses, small places of worship.'[272]

★

Delivered by *Kangaroo* in September 1853, the Cannans' house lived up to the promise that its package would contain all that was needed for it to be easily assembled in just a few hours. David's old friend the ship's carpenter 'who bolted from the ship and had to

20 *Jane Cannan: 'Back of our house'. A view across back gardens with a smaller outbuilding roofed in curved corrugated iron. As on the house's front, the iron windows are divided into four lights across, and three vertically, with the top row on a pivot. As Jane pointed out to relatives in Europe, the large suburban plot compensated for the modest interiors of these cottages. (Royal Historical Society of Victoria)*

skulk at first – for fear of being taken – turned up just in time to do our house'.[273] The interior needed rather more work – walls were generally lined with tongue and groove boards, then adorned with canvas or paper.

Jane and David bought the Pollocks' cast-off household goods to add to their own rugs, chairs, crockery, silver and pictures:

> We are lucky in having some furniture with us, for even the simplest little table answering to a deal one at home costs two pounds – Chests of drawers are unknown luxuries – and if you think shelves will do instead, you have to pay so much a foot for your board and 2/6 an hour to a man to come and put them up – It cost us between 5 and 6 pounds to fetch half of our boxes from the ship & 12/- for sending three of them from the office here – a distance of a mile or more through the town…boxes or packing cases out of which people make dressing tables and washstands can be got for 5/- a piece.[274]

After so many months' waiting, unpacking their boxes was a wonderful treat:

> All the actual things that we bought were 8 chairs two tables – and a stretcher for the servant – besides this we had cooking utensils and a few dinner dishes &c to buy – and almost everything else came out of David's big case – which contained his large easy chair in the centre – It was the greatest treat to unpack that case – How the candle sticks and salt cellars…and even a little hearth rug came out of it – to say nothing of all the silver spoons and the tea pot – That butter dish has been of the greatest use and comes on the table every day – I used to be afraid of getting worldly minded [but] I had so much pleasure in putting out the things – and putting them into the best places – The large easy chair and Agnes' American one look very well – and

we have a patent sofa which I invented myself and which
has been copied by two ladies – older colonists than myself!
It consists of a mattress covered with striped calico and laid
over two of my zinc boxes – with a flat pillow for head – and
a pillow and bolster like other sofas and a valance to hide the
boxes – All our boxes are converted into seats and dressing
tables except these two – and two which David and I keep
our clothes in – We put one box on another – the oftenest
wanted on the top and cover the whole with some sort of
dressing – and there is an article of furniture at once – and
the boxes got rid of – I think Berliners would do here very
well except that they would not like the small rooms.[275]

That life on a ship had moral and practical lessons for cabin
passengers, was much reiterated. 'Colonial' conditions legitimated and,
in the telling romanticised, what might have been somewhat shameful:

The voyage was capital preparation for Australia in many
respects…I think nothing of making the bed – and would
sweep out the room any day with pleasure.[276]

In their lodgings Jane declared that

we thought it quite natural for David to go and lie on the
bed when he came in here – as there was no sofa in the
parlour and we think a piece of print stretched at the end of
our curtainless four post bed makes a grand dressing room
for our dressing room in the ship was only two feet wide,
being the strip at the end of the bed curtained off.[277]

The respectable nineteenth century 'Home' epitomised a feminine
refuge for men from the world of competition and commerce.
However much Jane was aware that this ideal was unattainable for
most, and undesirable for some, she cannot but have been influenced
by the strength of the evangelical vision of what a home – and thus

a wife – should be. In contrast to the French trend for more family socialising in cafés and restaurants, and strolling in public spaces, England saw a growing trade in heavy velvet curtains to shield inhabitants from passers-by as family life and entertaining became more private and inward-looking.

Alongside this demarcation between public and private spheres was a firm distinction in the functions of a house's rooms. While to the Georgians rooms had been adaptable spaces, Victorian etiquette and home-making guides insisted that private spaces (bedrooms, the study) were for the family only. Servants' spaces (the kitchen, scullery and sleeping areas) were rooms that guests should not see, and other spaces (the morning room, dining room, and drawing room) were for the receiving of visitors. In reality many people lived in rather small houses and anxiously struggled to maintain the furnishings and protocols required for this ideal.[278] Jane's careful descriptions of Australian-style accommodation exemplify the compromises and contrasts. Their neighbours, the Jägers, fellow churchgoers and aspirant school teachers, had a large house with two parlours and five bedrooms which Jane later described as,

> furnished in Australian style – but very neat & comfortable – one iron stretcher without curtains – one chair one dressing table made of boxes covered with chintz one wash stand and a towel horse consisting of a cord stretched across the corner of the room from wall to wall – and Indian matting on the floor – Three of these rooms are outbuildings down one side of a sort of court – and the kitchen servants room and stable are down the other side.[279]

Jane had the task of being the 'angel', as the Victorians conceived it, in a tiny four-roomed house, which had a scullery at the back for the servant and an outside kitchen. Emigrants' houses designed by Morewood & Rogers and others were originally based on the cabins produced for the Californian miner. Now their interiors with separate bedrooms and parlour and carefully considered fittings implied a suitability for the respectable family-minded settler, a factor which drew a seal of approval from Mrs Chisholm.[280] Many Melbourne portable houses in fact were lived in by civil servants, builders, and tradesmen, rather than the labourer or pioneer in the bush.[281] Nevertheless, Jane faced quite a challenge, both practically and psychologically. She happily rose to it in her correspondence, telling Jeannette

> I will send you a sketch of our cottage by and bye for those lithographs that we had in Westmoreland do not give a good idea. Ours looks very clean and neat – of a good sort of light bluish tinge it is set far back on a tiny narrow piece of ground – and there is a grand wooden paling all round – six feet high – Fencing is very expensive here & we think ours very handsome – because it is made out of good broad packing cases boards instead of being made of barrel staves or anything of that sort. The house stands on rising ground, and looks across a church reserve…and a little to the left we have part of the village of Prahran with little shops and neat cottages with verandas…We are to have a nice garden in front and there is a capital yard behind so it may be a very pretty place in time. [I imagine…] the house covered with creepers and the paling hid behind roses and laburnums – white lilies – fuchsias and stocks &c, &c.[282]

Would she have preferred one of the little wooden houses which she drew and which belonged to the established settlers, their verandas richly hung with passion flowers and lydolichos? 'I always admire those' wrote Jane, 'but they suggest nothing but ants and mosquitos to David to say nothing of tarantulas and centipedes [and flies].'[283] Loyally she declared, she

> would not change [our house] for any in "the Colony" as I feel it so very much our own – having seen it rise on the very bare ground & form into a house over our head – I

felt like an oyster in a shell – We are thinking of painting and papering – Does not that sound grand? [284]

21 *Jane Cannan: 'Street scene with horse and cart'. The central house could be the Cannans', looking much more appealing in its leafy setting than when first constructed. If so, this would be Gardiner's Creek (now Toorak) Road. (National Library of Australia)*

While 'the house is being lined with metal so it will look rather funny till it is papered', Jane expected it would be 'a very snug little place'.[285] As Jane was to find, snug it was not in winter, but in the meantime David's enthusiasm for galvanised iron, and for Morewood & Rogers' ingenuity in packing all that a new household would need, was let loose; he wrote home:

[Our house] is galvanised tinned Iron outside & inside (being double) and is very comfortable, better than wood a great deal. It has a fence of galvanised wire, & a cistern of ditto, Washing tub, Buckets, Washstands & tables, not to speak of Iron bedsteads, & even knife rests which do quite as well as silver. Our agent at Adelaide even had a cradle made of it & I am going to have some picture frames made of it very soon. I have also a dish for feeding poultry.[286]

When Gardiner's Creek Road was re-cut and lowered, David

planned a new fence, not in wood like their neighbours', but of corrugated iron sheets with an iron door.[287]

Contrasting Jeannette's bourgeois standing in Berlin with her own, Jane qualified the basic little house by pointing out that its site was generous and its boundary fenced. The larger space compensated, then, for the lower status house:

> We are very lowly in our little cottage but we have a splendid piece of ground surrounding us – and can do what we like behind our high paling – ours is quite a village sort of life – and we know all our neighbours by sight and have hosts of children playing about the neighbourhood…David goes off in the morning about ½ past 8 or more – and gets back very punctually at 5 and hardly ever goes out again – our Sundays in general are pretty quiet too – going to the Scotch church in the morning and [because Harriet, the servant] goes off then to her friends we have early dinner…and I make tea.[288]

The stark little house and its quarter acre plot was cheerfully framed by Jane invoking cottage economy notions, perhaps remembering Sultan, the magnificent Cochin-China cock who paraded about Martineau's driveway.[289] She told Jeannette that she wanted to hear of her Berlin household, 'in return for which you shall be personally introduced to all the cocks and hens and ducks that we keep at Prahran – we have had a present of a cock already.'[290]

The inflated prices worried Jane, for, although thanks to Morewood & Rogers their house was rent-free, the housekeeping was daunting:

> I have been so little accustomed to think of having to buy thread, nails, cords, starch, salt, <u>water</u> & firewood that I imagine myself constantly stocking just for some trifle which I have not remembered to get in town.…If we had had rent to pay at the Melbourne rates we could not have lived on £350 a year even now I believe it will be impossible for if

22 Jane Cannan: 'Suburban street, Melbourne'. A street with a double Gothic gabled building on the right, possibly the South Yarra Club Hotel, on the south-east corner of Gardiner's Creek (now Toorak) Road and Punt Road, looking east. (National Library of Australia)

we have 50 or 60 a year to pay for ground rent – and 30 for a servant that with house rates will come to nearly 100 leaving 250 for provisions & nothing for clothes such as knee boots & waterproofs, which David will want for next wet season.[291]

★

Jane developed a 'nervous equilibrium' with Harriet, her servant, knowing she was fortunate to have one at all. In their lodgings, Mrs Kerr had produced breakfast,

eggs and meat to chose from with excellent baker's bread and good tea. Mrs Kerr manages to get up & brush the boots, and "set" the breakfast, frying chops and boiling eggs – in the most admirable manner and then sitting down to do hostess as if she had not lighted a fire, and brought hot water to our room besides all the rest. After breakfast…she sets to work again & I help a little. I generally wash the breakfast things in the parlour, & put them by in a corner on the floor where they are hid by the so called chiffoniere which is a box set on end and covered with hanging drapery – then she comes up to sweep and dust the room, which is covered with a sort of mosaic of carpeting, rather bad to brush because the little pieces are not sewed together.[292]

Now Jane and Harriet

work away together – She has a peculiar code of morals – and Irish habit of only speaking the truth when quite convenient – and much preferring to invent a few excuses even when she is not found fault with – She washes very fairly and takes a pride in the "master's shirts" and says "himself" could not wear a badly washed one – She is only a poor cook – but considerably better than her mistress – She gets at the rate of £30 a year but does not draw it at present – She rather neglects dress – and I sometimes have to give her a hint about her hair or a torn dress as I don't like the look of a slatternly girl to wait a dinner – She apologises and brushes up – On the other hand she does not like the look of a slatternly mistress – and always urges me to wear more petticoats and clean gowns – one day she passed through the room and noticed my collar which was I own very dirty – "Mrs Cannan! You have on a scandalous collar!" – says she!

She talks away to me all day quite familiarly – and I always soften a scolding with <u>We</u> have neglected those windows – <u>we</u> must really wash the sugar basin but at night when David is in – she keeps the door shut – & never expects me to do anything – She also seldom makes any observation to me before him unless some frog or bat or tarantula has excited her –

We should be sorry to lose her as we could hardly expect a better – and might easily get worse – She has a weakness about sweeping and dusting – neither of which things she can do decently or will do regularly – She likes a room to wait till it is thoroughly dirty before she sweeps it – and then she will not stoop but takes a long handled broom – I dust the parlour every morning while David gets up and do the bedrooms on those days that Harriet washes – I fold the clothes but let her wash and iron and carry to the mangle.[293]

Nevertheless, there was some keeping up of appearances: Mrs Pollock would not allow her daughters to answer the door though she had not been above doing so herself when they had no servant.[294] Again, however, we should be cautious of exaggerating the contrast with 'home'. As we have seen, Martineau made a point of respecting her servants' needs for time off and space of their own. Moreover, she had made it fashionable to take part in gardening, animal husbandry and preserving, which was just as well, given that the pull of industry was making it harder to get domestic servants at rates that the middle classes could afford. Many English women were therefore doing much of their household work alongside a single maid-of-all work though some, Cranford-style, pretended a life of serviced leisure.[295] The difference is that in Australia the situation could be reported openly, as an amusing scene from colonial life rather than an embarrassment.

★

Jane settled in; she had a black cat that purred on her knee, she taught drawing to the neighbours' children, and could

make or cause to be made, five different puddings, besides pies and tarts – I can make collared brawn out of shin of beef – and can turn out a mess of broth with some strength and colour in it. I am learning to be a judge of our potatoes – and can refuse a bad thing in a shop without apologising to the shopkeeper – finally I can sweep a room…and absolutely prefer washing at home.[296]

Reflecting on married life, Jane wondered whether her fellow newly-wed Jeannette felt at home buying wood and fish and potatoes and flour, and salt and pepper, and sardellen, and weiss brod, and what sort of caffee maschine you have got, and what you do all day, whether you grow methodical & keep accounts, whether the servant calls you gnädige Frau, and whether you ever feel as if you were the mistress of the house, or live in the idea that Emil has just asked you in and that you must go home to tea![297]

Housekeeping and dining – on something approximating to a familiar English diet – had become a routine, albeit one still novel enough, because of Jane's own contribution, to report home on:

We have a leg of mutton and a piece of roast beef every week and fill up the odd days with stewed chops and steaks – Now the weather is cool one joint lasts us two or three days and we ring the changes in hashed and cold &c…We sometimes have a beefsteak dumpling…For the second course we ring the changes on fruit pies and rice, with the addition of arrowroot blanc mange – We can make no pancakes or egg puddings because it is all I can do to get eggs enough to give David one for his breakfast – as my dear fowls are moulting.[298]

Now that the genteel had to support each other in practical ways, a welcome informality came into the Cannans' lives. Jane commented that people were more spontaneous about making calls. The Coopers (Mr Cooper was the head man at David's office) were neighbours. The two ladies' calls did not have the punctilious character (half an hour at most, on specified days and times) of those etiquette minefields at home – as we see from Jane's exclamation marks:

You ask after my friendships [I go to Mrs Cooper] two or three times a week – I pass her house on the way to the shops at Prahran – or to Mrs Hicks – we exchange colonial civilities. I knit socks for the baby or go to help her to make a cupboard while she bakes me a seed loaf in her stove – or a currant one – if I will pick the currants!!!![299]

And she reiterated the informality of calls to Agnes Cannan, whereby

It is quite the custom to set lunch before everyone who calls…If there is nothing in the house but bread and butter that is brought in – but generally people have anchovy paste – jam – or preserved ginger for such occasions.[300]

And some were boldly enterprising in behaviour and style:

Some of us went to the Exhibition of Fine Arts – Miss Pollock, Mrs Blanchard & I went to see the pictures, which are sent to a room in the Mechanics Institution to be exhibited by public spirited gentlemen who just send what they have – with a small sprinkling of views of the country by some of the artists in the town. Mrs Blanchard rode in from the country on horseback – having forded the Yarra with some difficulty as the water was high, she is about 40 and has hair as white as Mamma's which she wears in short tidy ringlets, and no cap – in her hat she wore…little cock feathers – but for all that looks very nice, and has very quiet manners.[301]

Jane did remark that while people were not so different from home, the subjects of conversation, in a population of which more than half had arrived in recent years, were a little different:

You generally begin with "And how long have you been in the Colony" – If the customer is a recent comer – you then compare length of passage, behaviour of Captain, number of storms, heat of the tropics and bills of fare on the voyage – if not you get to talking of tents – iron house – wood stone & brick house – some have great prejudices against one – some against another – and everyone gives you their experience as if they were quite sure you would believe them…ladies always compare the price of the last load of wood – and gloat over a good load that burns well "without blowing" as Miss Martineau might say over a Westminster Review.[302]

It is worth reiterating that Jane already had models for a relatively informal social life. Her brother Louis enjoyed the conviviality among his engineer colleagues both in England and the USA. While he had literary tastes and was at home in drawing rooms, Louis gravitated to more informal company. He had been overjoyed to meet the actors who had travelled on *City of Manchester* with him after their performance in Cincinnati, and in Canada 'heard more that was new & interesting from the lumbermen & emigrant or native labourer & mechanic than from the fashionable of New York'.[303] And Scottish David, with a Nonconformist's disdain for worldly status, his shaking of the servant's hand at his wedding, his preference for the company of the ship's carpenter and Mr Plant, the mate, to the 'prosy' Mr Campbell, was ready for Melbourne's class revolution.

★

With such a scattered family, news of Jane's marriage had travelled slowly. Nevertheless, by October, she had heard from Louis who could now imagine David as

a "shadow of a youth with fair hair and a scotch accent" – Louise is more complementary – says he must be good if I have him – while Uncle Charles clears his throat across from Valparaiso – and says as all that is said about Mr Cannan is so very satisfactory there is every reason to hope that the marriage will be a happy one.[304]

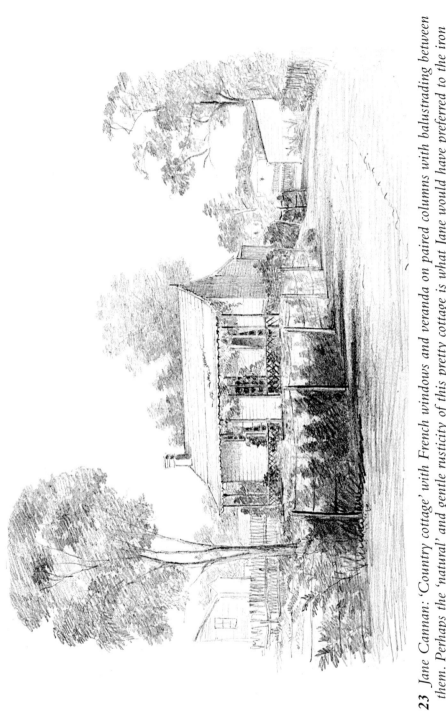

23 Jane Cannan: 'Country cottage' with French windows and veranda on paired columns with balustrading between them. Perhaps the 'natural' and gentle rusticity of this pretty cottage is what Jane would have preferred to the iron house. (National Library of Australia)

It was to her sister-in-law Mary Cannan that Jane confided the relief and freedom she felt at being away from family demands:

I feel it good to be in a place where no one knows that I had a history or a former life – The voyage was an excellent break, and if we went back tomorrow I should still feel that coming away had cured that sort of restlessness and irritability that latterly rather teased me – and often led me into talking more nonsense…I don't think David knows that rattling nonsensical side of my character at all…

I don't know what to say about David except…he looks a little [better] for having his cheeks better filled up and if he improves at this rate, will be quite handsome in another year…As for me I am wonderfully improved in my dress – "though I say it that should not do it" and so David means to keep the books tidy in the house and not to let me lay anything on the sofa…but we shall see and as I said before I don't mean to fret myself about it…the uncertainty of life is so often brought before one and I know that the one may be taken & the other left any day, so why be too anxious for the future. If David gets on well it will be all right and if he falls sick I should be better situated in regard to ensuring something here than at home as one can get lodgers…

I am surprised at your turning musical…That wretch David has not much interest in him & cannot understand the effect it has on others – but I know no music equal to his voice when he says my Jane my darling my cherished wife – & with that piece of what he would call sentimental rubbish (though he knows better) I must sign off & am your very affectionate sister[305].

There were times of nostalgia for home, which for David meant Galloway rather than the hated Manchester. Perhaps the sheer numbers and success of Scottish immigrants in Australia, already littered with Scots place names, strengthened David's pride in his identity and forebears. On Sundays there was the 'Scotch' (Presbyterian) church in the mornings, and in the evenings, 'David sits in the armchair – and I on the footstool by the fire – and we are sure to talk of the Grampians or the Shiel or Carsphairn' while looking at the little family daguerreotypes and photographs, and perhaps some drawings, that lived in the travelling desk.[306]

Jane doesn't mention nostalgia of her own. In general at this stage David and Jane professed themselves satisfied with life in Melbourne, partly because they were accumulating money, partly because the climate suited David's health, and perhaps because, far from leaving people behind, many acquaintances and relatives such as the Maitlands and Cullens were also there. As was Martineau's former servant, 'the mesmeric' Jane Arrowsmith, who had called with flowers. She 'is a sort of cook and housekeeper at a nice house a short distance from us – She came to bring me the Ambleside news and informed me that a certain cart driver of the name of Fisher – to whom [she] was supposed to be attached (by Miss Martineau) was coming out.'[307]

★

In March 1854, nearly a year after her marriage, and drying out the house after the autumn rains, Jane wrote to Jeannette congratulating her on her 'prospects'. She rationalised her own childlessness as a blessing given the frightful infant mortality, for 'It is truly grievous to hear of the bereaved parents – in many cases without one child left.'[308]

Nevertheless, soon after this she was pregnant. But times were changing. David was very poorly in the July and August winter cold, and he was anxious to be free of the need to work. The excitement over the diggings had died down, and with it the business boom. Melbourne was settling into a hum-drum existence albeit as a new and wealthy city. 1854 saw an exhibition, to move on to Paris, in which Morewood & Rogers' galvanised tinned iron was displayed. The sleek clippers, and *Great Britain* and other steamers, together with the overland route, were reducing the time lapse between Britain and Melbourne. The city was now establishing a university, and the state a museum and library. A little railway now

24 Jane Cannan: 'Group of houses'. An attractive home with a settled appearance showing Jane's growing appreciation of the Australian style - a hip-roofed house with striped and trellised veranda and other buildings in the background. (National Library of Australia)

reached Sandridge: 'how different people must feel who arrive now and come up by train in five minutes', rather than walking into a raw, remote new world, struggling with baggage and writing desk, as had she and David.[309]

EIGHT

Heavy failure in the iron trade

In March 1855 Jane informed her mother-in-law that a thriving Louisa had been born the previous month, and that she was being helped by the new servant, Catherine, and by Mrs Cooper (whose two children had died).

> I am very well and able to carry her about the country in true colonial style. I felt rather nervous at first when the nurse left, and I had been under my own charge altogether, but now she is growing more hardy & will bear handling – and can cry for half an hour without any disastrous consequences, and I do not go so often to see whether she is dead when she is asleep – She is said to be more like David than me, but I think there is nothing but the light complexion & fair hair to judge by as yet – She is a plump strong little thing – and very good and contented on the whole – David has got her a "perforated zinc"! cradle and she sleeps in that with a gauze thrown over her – safe from the flies and mosquitoes which have been very annoying the last few weeks…
>
> I send you a sketch of Miss Louisa Cannan in her metal cradle – as I cannot draw faces you must take the portrait of the cradle instead of that of the child.[310]

Their neighbours, however, Jane continued, had moved into a smaller house, and several friends, Dr McCrae among them, were losing their employment or having cuts in incomes. 'Practicing economy' was back. A few days later the *Argus* reported, in its business news from London:

HEAVY FAILURE IN THE IRON TRADE: A large failure was announced on 4th January in the iron trade, the firm being that of Messrs Morewood and Rogers, with liabilities for £180,000. They represent their assets as capable of realising, ultimately, with good management, £280,000, but, having been disappointed with respect to remittances from Australia, as well as in obtaining a further advance of £30,000 which they had anticipated from a provincial house…it has become necessary for them to suspend.[311]

David was being pursued by the Union Bank of Australia which, having advanced credit to him against Morewood & Rogers' bills of exchange, found they had not been honoured. While the Supreme Court of Victoria would issue a restraining order on the bank the following year, it was surely a year of pressure for David.[312]

By 1855 Victoria was inundated with portable iron buildings exported from Britain. Morewood & Rogers were not alone: John Walker, Hemming, Bellhouse and others had joined the rush to supply the colony. Meanwhile housing shortages had eased as domestic construction and manufacturing got underway. Suddenly the *Argus* was full of bargains: houses and galvanised building materials, implements and household goods, flooded a buyers' market.[313]

The London trustees of Morewood & Rogers' estate, represented by John Walker, assured David that he could continue with his original contract while he attempted to dispose of their stock. £750 per annum and the rent-free iron house were still his. Walker acknowledged that he had quite a task, with duties to perform to a large body of creditors.[314] Morewood & Rogers, as a large firm with an international trade, was able to begin paying a dividend to creditors late in 1855 (having liquidated property in Australia, and premises and stock in London, and cancelled the purchase of an estate in Glamorganshire in Wales), and to resume trading as Morewood & Co. The name was good, good enough to gain the huge contract for the new Indian telegraph system, their galvanised wire 'strong enough for the immense numbers of monkeys who will sit on it.'[315]

It seems that Pollock had finally become a partner in the original firm – he had been disappointed that he had not been accepted as such before his first departure for Adelaide. Walker's letter to David refers to discussing the Australian business with him, and Pollock may have had a part in the restructuring of the firm. While problems with iron buildings had been revealed (as they had in California) of poor insulation in heat or cold, and of fire risk due to the great temperatures they could reach (contradicting claims of fire-proof qualities), manufacturers' eyes were already on other markets. After all, the prefabricated building had its *raison d'être* in portability, in its speedy arrival in a destination where its use might be temporary. Now instant hospitals, stables and stores were needed for Britain's war in Crimea. Other regions offered opportunities, including southern America and South Africa, and schools, chapels and shooting lodges were dispatched to Wales and Scotland.[316] The manufacture and export to Australia of galvanised iron building components continued apace, however, and in Australia corrugated iron roofing sheets, verandas shaded by graceful curves painted in bright stripes, became an iconic image of domestic architecture.

★

Adolphe Claude, Jeannette's older brother, wrote in July 1854 from Valparaiso to his cousin Jane. He had heard both of her marriage and arrival in Australia, and of Jeannette's marriage and arrival in Berlin.[317] Later that year he became custom-house clerk in Myers Bland & Co, his younger brother Charles having just entered their Liverpool office. A Doering son, John, from Liverpool was also in Chile, a clerk in another house, soon to be joined by Hans Chodowieki, a Berlin cousin. Social life was restricted to a small number of expatriate merchant colleagues, mainly single men, the Claudes' bilingualism widening their circle to German colleagues.

Adolphe and some other young clerks had stayed at one point with Uncle Charles Claude in his large house:

> To him I think it must be an agreeable change, for a short time to have company tho' it interferes with the diet he usually keeps (viz only eggs for breakfast & beefsteak for dinner) as he gets tempted by the good things he gives us, which however I trust will do him no harm. His only companion before was a tame canary-bird that flies about the room during breakfast & a dog to accompany him in his walks & at dinner. [318]

In October 1854 Uncle Charles died while suffering from dysentery. Adolphe and Dr Thomas, principal of Myers Bland, arranged the funeral, attended by most of the Englishmen of the place. His gravestone, according to Adolphe, stated simply that he was born in 1800 in Berlin, was a merchant, and died in Copiapó.

Charles' will, in a certified translation from the Spanish, bequeathed his estate – funds in England and Chile, his property, furniture and ornaments – to his nine nieces and nephews.[319] The widows Mrs Claude and Jane's aunts Minne and Henriette now had annuities, profitably invested in the new Copiapó railroad. Mary, Jane, Louise and Louis, like their five first cousins, inherited just over thirty thousand Chilean dollars, which roughly translated to £6,000 which, if invested, would yield an annual income of £300.

Adolphe was executor with Mr Thomas. Given the distances involved and the slowness of shipping between India, the USA, Australia, Prussia, England and Chile, the work of settling the legacies was complex. In June 1855, however, he wrote to Jane to say that her money was to be paid to Messrs Gibbs & Co in Valparaiso who had her power of attorney.

Meanwhile, wrote Adolphe, Louis was in New York, saying he would be in England soon, before going to India to bring Louisa's children home. He was hatching the dream that Uncle Charles would now make possible: the purchase of land at the beautiful Devil's Lake in Wisconsin to build his homestead.

Jane and David could surely now fulfil their own dream: the Westmoreland cottage would be a comfortable one, they could have more than one servant, and David could live as a gentleman. The Morewood & Rogers tasks having diminished, Jane told Mary Cannan the following year that David was now:

> a gentleman at large only going into town two or three times a week and then only for a few hours – coming back in time to have a walk with me in the afternoon – The weather is very pleasant for walking…then we read in the evenings or go in to some of our neighbours to tea – as there is more time to be sociable now, than when he was so busy & so tired with his day's work. [320]

★

Jane's marriage settlement had placed her money in the hands of two trustees: Uncle Charles and Louis. David's younger brother Thomas Robert Story Cannan, described as 'merchant of Manchester' in the documents replaced the deceased Charles. The trustees represented each side of the marriage, and, if all went amicably, gave David and Jane a say in how the funds were to be managed.

Instead, anger and resentment suddenly permeate the correspondence. The wider family now seemed united only by the further dividends and divisions of remnants of the estate. Adolphe, in the eye of the storm, crafted diplomatic but quietly exasperated letters. David wrote wildly to Jeannette that

> Jane says you need not write if you are going to blow her up as she has had enough of that already – <u>enough</u> indeed! I offered to resign in favour of Mrs Claude…seeing that she

was so anxious to interfere with our affairs and propose as soon as I get to England to become a member of the "Anti poke your nose into other people's business Society"![321]

Jane's more measured account of the times to Agnes Cannan told her how anxious they had been to return to Britain, but

When M & R accepted the resignation in January, David was for packing immediately and awaiting the "successor" with corded trunks – & though I was pretty philosophical just then – I was in a great fidget to be off when David took dysentery. Now we are quite tired of expecting anything to be settled – and look upon ourselves as colonists for the time being – I suppose you will know before this whether they are sending the Successor or expecting David to stop.[322]

Clearly David and Jane were in a frustrating limbo, the uncertainty over his position with Morewood & Rogers a consequence of long intervals between writing and receiving mail. Perhaps the gnawing fear of declining health underlay some of the bitterness in the Cannans' letters to Jeannette? But far, far worse was the death of their much loved 'nicest little darling that ever was' from dysentery in November 1855. David told his mother:

[Louisa's] funeral was on Tuesday afternoon. We had at it Revd Mr Corrie, Mr Hicks, Dr McCrae…and three of my own men. She was buried at the St Kilda Cemetery in the Presbyterian part – a very nice place overlooking the sea with plenty of trees…We know she is better where she is but it is hard to bear for all that – & my dear Jane is very desolate without her Louisa…I was only back from Adelaide a fortnight on Monday last & I was out in one of the most violent hurricanes ever seen on this coast – a heavy sea struck the steamer & carried away the bulwarks, ships boats, galley, binnacle &c, smashed in the cabin windows. [But] my little Louisa was spared to me then & was so jolly & so improved, you cannot tell how delighted I was to get back to my wife & daughter. And we have to be thankful for the good health Jane has always had since she came here – She is much younger like than when she was married & has fewer grew hairs – & I never saw her look so nice as she did tonight when I took her for a walk to see the grave of our lost Louisa – that is lost to us for this world only.[323]

Jane, writing to her mother a month after the death, her amusing irony displaced by a dreadful sense that her temporary blessing had been too good to be true, could only say:

It is four weeks today since our darling died and we seem as yet to miss her worse and worse every day...I was in Melbourne today and saw hundreds of babies and God would have spared her to us if He had seen fit – The Lord gave and the Lord has taken away and blessed be the name of the Lord who gave her such a happy little life and us such comfort and blessing in having her – still we miss her by night & by day – evening & morning – fair weather & foul – everything was considered in reference to her and now the cool wind blows & the sun goes down and we have no little girl to [share] our meals, & get up & go to bed without our little comfort to look at – who seemed to fill our hearts and thoughts and minds & now all our care and love is changed into an attempt to be unselfish & feel satisfied that it was for her good that this precious thing went before she knew what sorrow or suffering were.[324]

No child and no Morewood & Rogers now to hold them in Australia. Uncle Charles' money made choices possible. But it seems they had bought their house so needed to sell it before they could leave, and perhaps they were fearful of losing money on what had seemed like a good investment at the time. They hoped to sail in December so that the English winter would be avoided. Of this they were reminded by the Melbourne winter in the iron house:

> It really is very cold here just now in the houses – it cannot be said to be cold out of doors, as people do not require top coats or warm gloves – and if the houses were like English houses, it would not be cold inside either…
>
> It makes me feel rather strange when people come to look at this place with a view to buying it – if it should be sold soon we should go into lodgings here or perhaps at Brighton which is very pleasant in the summer – though rather cold & comfortless at present – We shall not have much difficulty in disposing of our furniture – half of it being composed of boxes – we can just pack the other half into them & send them to the warehouse to lie till we are ready to sail – Our chairs are literally on their last legs – and the tables have been bespoken some time – The carpets have done good service, and will last out our time, and we are half inclined to bring back David's easy chair with us (as) it has been a great comfort to us, & it reminds us of our little pet, who was nursed in it – The pictures too we shall take with us – and the books & all our pretty wedding presents – But there is time enough yet to think of packing – for no one seems inclined to buy the house in a hurry…
>
> There were two public holidays last week the first & second of July – the 1st is the regular annual holiday for the independence of Victoria, and the 2nd was for the peace – unfortunately the 2nd which was the grandest day – was so wet that all the pleasure was spoiled. We spent the first day at Hawthorne with the Wrights – and took such a long walk with them besides walking home at night that David was knocked up and had to lie in bed next day.[325]

The Cannans, now fearful of cold and anxious about travelling, were cheered by a visit by David's good-natured cousin Archie Cullen, a sheep farmer, probably in the Moreton Bay area:

We made a sort of holiday time of it, and went to Geelong for one night, & took a trip to Brighton, another day – eating our lunch on the shore – and went out to tea <u>four</u> times, which was tolerable gaiety for us – besides all the chat and the discussion of the old jokes, which I only half understood the point before – I expected a much rougher sort of individual, and was quite surprised to find that not only did he <u>not</u> smoke – but that he presented quite a drawing room appearance and put David's old hat so much to the blush – that he had to buy a new one immediately – He wears a beard & moustache, but is tanned a fine rich coffee colour – but does not otherwise look like a bushman…

He gave me more idea than I ever had before, of the country, and has left me the old map that he travelled down with – He is so used to riding, that he did not like walking at first, but got a little better used to it afterwards – He was almost as fond of the sofa as David, and used to practice ingenious arts to get David off it & when he could not succeed he used to lie on the hearth rug & tell us long stories of the blacks and how they would work for him for months, and how sometimes he had been left on the station without any whites whatever for a time – and had to depend on the natives altogether…Archie says the natives cut back for him & roof buildings, kill game, catch fish, cook, & wait on him, two boys were <u>given</u> to him – and he kept them some time – the women will do anything about a house and it is well to be on good terms with them – as white servants are scarce – He says all the blacks near his place, young and old, know him – and that when he goes back there will be a great shouting and rushing about, and that they will all crowd round him to ask what he has seen "behind the setting of the sun" – [He seems] to have a sort of affection for them, quite different to the feeling with which he regards the white shepherds and bullock drivers, who work the whole year for their thirty pounds & then travel down to the nearest public house and drink it all in a week or less.

He seemed to think nothing of riding seventy or eighty miles in a day to fetch a doctor in an emergency – and as to being thrown from his horse or being left hanging on by the arms in a branch that he could not pass under, he considered it a mere trifle...I always forget the great heat, and thought he seemed to have a very pleasant life of it... but it would not suit everybody, and to begin with a man must have a very decided taste for horsemanship & outdoor life...

Archie went with us to see the grave of our little pet and I was glad for any one belonging to David to see it before we left the country.[326]

Jane's curiosity about Australia re-emerged. She regretted that travel beyond the settlements was so difficult, and 'must own that I was greatly disappointed when Mr Hicks' horse would not go and spoiled our intended excursion to Anderson's creek sixteen miles off'. [327] She was disappointed that she had seen few native people, and perhaps she had discussed their situation with Webb who, on his work on the roads and bridges around Port Fairy, had been appalled at the degradation inflicted on them by 'civilised' man.[328] Pollock had noticed the cleverness with which the aboriginal people around Sydney managed their bark canoes, but he saw those of Adelaide, who wandered around the town wearing 'the least possible quantity of clothes', as an apathetic people. [329]

★

As we know from her drawings of the Bishop's Palace and the Collegiate Institution (St Peters), Jane got to Adelaide, and a journey to Sydney is mentioned. Then, after a tour of Tasmania (David 'sick

25 *Jane Cannan: 'Large house surrounded by trees', in fact one a two-storey Gothic house, and on the right a single-storey house with a wing apparently roofed in Morewood & Rogers tiles. In drawing these graceful houses, two residents in conversation under the long veranda, had Jane been dreaming of settling in Australia? (National Library of Australia)*

and furious' at Morewood when he saw fine stone houses roofed in 'beastly shingles'), they booked onto a steamer for the journey home, via the overland route through Egypt.[330]

This would be very different from the primitive conditions on *Hempsyke*. And in that short time, Melbourne had continued its rapid evolution from frontier town:

> Any one arriving now would not find it so very different from England…Schools are more plentiful & there is not the same difficulty of getting children amongst companions in their own rank as there are now schools for all sorts – Indeed in a general way it has almost become the fashion to run down England as much as they used to run down "the Colony" when we first came – and everyone says to us "Are you not sorry to be leaving?" At least all gentlemen say so…
>
> The only difficulty will be to compress what we want into a small compass – as they do not allow much luggage – We shall have to pay more attention to dress and etiquette on the steamer than we did in our ship coming when the rule was that the gentlemen had a clean shirt every Sunday – and shaved once a week – and blacked their boots also once a week – and the ladies – there being only one besides myself did just what they pleased. I understand we shall have to dress for dinner every day and the ladies will retire after dinner &c &c &c in the highest style of fashion to a drawing room with a piano – instead of retiring as Mrs Campbell and I did occasionally to my cabin – where we placed footstools on the bed and tucked up our feet, to keep them warm.

And, Jane continued, as to the little ugly iron house where she had briefly known happiness,

> The young man who has bought this place has begun to beautify it already by planting young trees in the front – He lives at present with his father & mother – but is to be

married in a few months though he is only 21 – He means to add two brick rooms to the end of the house – and leave the old part as it is.[331]

NINE

Smoothing the descent to the grave: Madeira

Tuberculosis, known to the Victorians as phthisis or consumption, accounted for around one in seven British deaths in the mid-nineteenth century. Generally thought of as inherited, it was not until 1882 that the German scientist Robert Koch demonstrated that the condition was caused by a bacillus. Ironically the momentous announcement, which meant that TB would now be recognised as an infectious disease, was made at a meeting of the Berlin Physiological Society whose eminent president was Emil du Bois Raymond.[332]

A persistent cough, breathlessness, loss of appetite, bloody phlegm, pallor, fever, lassitude, night sweats and a general sense of being unwell are the symptoms of TB. It can remain latent, activated only when the immune system is weakened. It can wax and wane in a person, progressing very slowly or rapidly (as in galloping consumption). Advanced TB is associated with hoarseness of voice due to the affected larynx, with difficulty in swallowing and pulmonary haemorrhages. Jane must have known what was the matter with the young David Cannan, son of Thomas whose premature death had all the signs of consumption. What she would not have fully understood was the risk she ran in living in close proximity to him.

Victorian doctors, well aware of the progress of this dreadful disease with its fifty percent mortality rate, could only treat its symptoms. When they saw the last stages approaching the best they could do was to recommend – to those who could afford it – a warm climate to 'smooth the descent to the grave'.[333] Italy had been the preferred country until the instability that followed the 1848 revolution. French Mediterranean resorts, such as Hyères and Nice, and the Swiss mountain sanatoria were beginning to come into their own, but in 1860 Portuguese Madeira was, for the British invalid, the resort of choice. One of the many guide books to this balmy, verdant island's English boarding houses, reading rooms and doctors sought to allay fears that the streets of Funchal were over-populated by invalids in distressingly advanced conditions. Indeed, it continued, the majority walked about in such a lively manner that it was difficult to believe they were patients.[334]

★

Once returned to London in 1857, Jane told her mother-in-law that the doctor 'has ordered David a blister [a hot poultice designed to draw off inflammation] the effect of which he is to see in ten days.' [335] Jane, however, was herself unwell, telling Jeannette optimistically that:

> We have a visit to pay in Scotland – and the doctor still keeps us uncertain, as we have to see him once in three weeks – and do not know before hand what he may recommend but my desire is just to live as quietly as possible without any excitement – Even pleasurable excitement is a trouble to me just now but as long as I can eat & sleep as I do there cannot be much the matter with me physically – and I dare say I shall be quite vigorous by the time I have to take up house...I shall hear how you are through [my sister] Louise – who is in great trouble herself about the Indian insurrection.[336]

Writing to David in October of their good Manchester lodgings, the landlady being 'very kind and quiet and a capital cook', Jane referred ominously to the doctor being 'better satisfied with my tongue yesterday than he has yet been...I am longing to have you back'.[337] Jane surely went to Manchester's epoch-making Exhibition of Art Treasures, during which Mrs J. McConnel entertained sixty-nine visitors, though David's illness meant that he and Jane missed seeing Queen Victoria and the grand review. [338] In a purpose-built iron and steel hall, no larger art exhibition had ever been organised. Special trains brought entire firms of mill-workers complete with brass bands. Manchester, still an over-crowded city with inadequate sewerage and water supply, high levels of infectious disease and low education levels among its working class, was nevertheless reinventing itself with grand civic buildings and the means to relate the best in art to industrial design.[339]

Some of Jane's old gaiety bubbles through in her letters. She had returned just in time to bid Pollock and his mother goodbye as they 'are going back to Australia & sail on Monday!!!!'[340] She enjoyed a pleasant stay in an Irish country house, admired the Galloway countryside in Scotland, and sounds comfortable with the Cannan/Kennedy extended family for whom she drew their property at Castramont and the village of Carsphairn. She visited the cousinhood of Cullens and Maitlands. In London she walked in the parks and was deep in *The Daisy Chain*, Charlotte M. Yonge's highly successful novel of a family of motherless children engaging in charitable work.

Richmond was then a quiet, elegant village, within easy reach of London by train. Here the Cannans took lodgings, supported by the ever-friendly Mrs Chadwick. Mary Cannan was nearby, teaching her cousin Robert Cannan's children while he was participating in the Crimean War. Charles, named after Uncle Charles, was born in August 1858, and christened by David's cousin Frank Cannan, Presbyterian chaplain to the military in Aldershot.

While Louisa had had her 'little exacting habits', and would 'clap hands so prettily & always looked so pleased when she had found out what we wanted her to do', Charles was remarkably strong and sturdy, 'needing socks made on a much larger scale', and 'screamed and roared tremendously'. [341]

The death of one of Jeannette's children in 1857 had reopened some of the old intimacy. Jane had written to her expressing her sympathy, adding that she and Tante Minne 'were among my best comforters when our own dear child was taken from us, you were amongst the few who seemed to know what we were suffering…The world seems changed, death seems the chief work of life.'[342]

Yet Jane still harboured a grievance that while her sister Louise (and her husband) had been allowed by Louis and Adolphe to have control of her inheritance, altering her original marriage settlement, she, Jane, had not. She wrote bitterly to Jeannette, who was well-off and so probably less exercised by the issue:

> I can however congratulate you that you have been more fortunate – and hope that your castles in the air will all flourish – and that you will soon have a little model summer house in Potsdam and plenty of nephews and nieces in Valparaiso – and that Emil will discover some new nerves – and Dick will blend the scientific and the mercantile and Ellen and Claude will speak seven languages.[343]

In the same letter Jane described herself as having been driven out from her family home, it having been less of a trial to be at the Antipodes than 'a home which is no home'. The rift with her mother, sisters and brother was clearly deep.

Adolphe was still trying to reassure Jane that her treatment over the legacy was not out of line with her and David's requests. Perhaps David had fired another enraged salvoe in his direction – or at Messrs Gibbs, Bright & Co who were handling the English end of the transactions. We know from Webb's account that David could be sarcastic. Perhaps his illness had begun tipping him into unreasonable anger. A fragment of a letter reminiscing well after these years, and probably from Agnes Cannan, wife of David's brother James, said:

> [Jane] and I were great friends, they lived with us for three months after they returned from Australia so I really knew her better than anyone in the family. She was the very sweetest creature possible, indeed too much so for her own

comfort, for she never allowed herself to express a thought or wish contrary to her husband's and in spite of a kind heart he had the most wrong headed notions of people & things so he always said "Jane thinks as I do". She often said to me "if I could only let them (her people) know I don't, it would be less hard for all."[344]

In a conciliatory letter to Jane, regretting that dissension had entered the family, Adolphe hoped that their friendship could continue as before.[345] His next letter suggested this might be difficult, and that his fortunes had changed. He become a partner at Myers, Bland & Co, and:

Your husband calls me an unfortunate bachelor, and is quite right, but I now hope not to remain one much longer, for I am engaged to be married to Miss Marion Schwager, who I need not say is a very nice, sensible girl... The celebration of the independence of this country on the 18th September was spoilt by a row in which the Governor of the province was shot, but everything is quiet for the present at least.[346]

Adolphe's marriage to Marion Schwager would make him an even more prosperous man: she was the heir to the great Schwager coal enterprise in Chile.

★

So the friendly, handsome, unconventional David was becoming frail, blustering and intolerant. A photograph in his middle years shows a sunken-faced and wasted figure, whose horizons were reduced to short walks in Bournemouth on England's south coast to which he and Jane now moved. He was becoming the sort of man whose love for 'his dear Jane, his cherished wife' could not extend to imagining her side of things. An added twist was a disagreement over a daughter of Dr Lewis (of Guildford) who lived with Mrs Claude and Mary at

Broadlands. There are hints that she was illegitimate, but if so why should David have whipped himself into a state of rage over the matter?

By September in 1858 clouds were gathering. Writing to David's sister Agnes to thank her for a cape she had made for the baby, Jane referred to having had 'a sort of nervous fever for some weeks…I am very much improved now – and the doctor thinks change will do the rest.'[347]

David looked around Devon. He did not like the resort of Torquay very much – too exposed to the east winds and not so hot as expected. He then went to Barnstaple in north Devon but thought the County Wicklow scenery superior and didn't think much of the air either.[348] Jane and David shifted to Poole, near Bournemouth; to David's sister Agnes she described their lodgings, which took invalids who arrived during the autumn:

> After that according to our landlady there is not a "hattic" to be had in the place – In April or May these people leave, & then comes the "slack time" till people come with their families for bathing, when the place is likely to be pretty full again…
>
> We cannot however delude ourselves into thinking it a cheap place, as Mrs Falls, who has kept strict accounts for a large family, says it is just the same as London West End Prices…Mr Falls is not the white neckcloth London style of doctor at all, little and countrified, wearing woollen stockings & shoes, & nursing his foot on his knee in a manner far below the Great Hassal, he comes once a week, and I am taking the cod liver oil on a mixture of his which seems to do my bowels good – My cough is much better, & I can walk rather better.[349]

Soon Jane had to relinquish much of the care of Charlie, who loved 'his Papa who has been his patient nurse maid ever since he was born & has now to bear all the brunt of the weaning as I am not allowed to lift him at all.'[350] Going to Madeira for the winter was advised. She thanked Jeannette for her wish for good lodgings

> as we are rather dependant on them for comfort in a strange place – especially as it will be <u>board and lodging</u> – and we may meet another set of lodgers at meals, however we are very philosophical and as long as no one snubs Charlie or stints him of his baby meals, & as long as no one scrubs my bedroom floor or puts me into damp sheets, we do not complain.
>
> We are taking some letters of introduction with us & our Doctor here has promised me a medical letter to Dr Lund there so that we shall know better how I am progressing, than if I went as a new patient. We are to have a letter to Mrs Lund too – and Drs wives are very often very agreeable people…If all goes well we might return at the end of May.[351]

Poor Jane felt old, though only thirty-seven. As she watched her cousin Dick, David, and Charlie 'representing the active world, she knew there was no longer occasion for Cousin Jane to come in with a chess board or a water colour box as she used to do.' Charlie, ' a bit of a pedant & likes order and uniformity', was 'very fond of David who always has to go to him when he is in trouble'.[352]

David got the baggage to Southampton, for a sailing delayed by stormy weather. Sarah, the servant, busied herself grinding up biscuits for Charlie's shipboard food, and Jane, now dependent on a respirator, sewed a pinafore and dressing gown for him. On board there would be

> a cow and a doctor – and we have a box of medicine from our druggist in case of emergencies…I have been interrupted several times, and it is now bed time – there are rockets going up for Guy Fawkes day – David has got home from Southampton very tired and hungry – We wish you all a merry Christmas and a happy New Year –[353]

After a week or so's steaming on the *Clyde*, David reported to his mother their safe arrival in Funchal, the capital:

> We are getting on very fairly as we are very comfortably located [with] Miss Wardross,…with a parlour & two bed rooms…We have had Dr Lund twice – he was here this morning & is not coming again for a fortnight – he said that Mr Fall's treatment was to be continued & that we did very right to leave England as the winter would not do for Jane at all. [354]

The curious household consisted of ten boarders. Charlie was not the only child – there was also an infant of a young widow whose husband had died six months formerly. Mr Gough, who shared a liking for books with David was, with Jane, one of the four invalids in the house:[355]

> We invalids spend the day in getting fresh air & eating meals and resting – I seldom leave the grounds as they are very pleasant – and there is no donkey chair or gig for me here – I tried horse back but could not manage it and I dislike the hammocks and palanquins which are used for invalids – as I feel so helpless in them – Cars or sledges drawn by oxen are rather rough conveyances – and boating makes me sick, this is however no great matter as we have a large garden extending to the rock overhanging the water, and a verandah with a view of the sea – where we can walk or sit, and a little private parlour where we have a sofa and easy chair – and can lie with the window open…
>
> By the bye the greatest part of the garden is laid out in a plantation of cactus – the ugliest crop imaginable for the cultivation of the Cochineal – which with sugar cane has taken the place of cultivation of the vine – The hills are very picturesque, but we have not penetrated into them, and they are so high & rise so directly out of the sea that we feel rather flies stuck on a wall than anything else. Those,

however, who can take excursions on horseback are I believe well repaid – Invalids are generally recommended to avoid all excitement & for myself I am obliged to do so…and found that the least bustle made me feel either so weak or so hysterical or so something that I seemed to lose the power of breathing and must either faint or cry – Once here however I can be pretty quiet and the daily habit of dressing for meals and facing the rest of the household seems to strengthen my nerves though I constantly drop my fork or do something dreadful of that kind – The gentlemen feel the want of daily papers very much.[356]

By May, the Cannan family had settled in. Charlie, in print frocks, flannel vests and Holland jackets with hats trimmed with white muslin to keep the sun off, played with the other infant and the doctor's son. He endured frightening lancings of his gums and mustard poultices, running from any hint of the doctor's voice or horse. Having been a singularly quiet child, he at last began talking, and picked up Portuguese from the hammock men, in whose company he spent considerable time pottering about the garden and slithering on the precipitous slopes.[357]

David, while a chronically sick man, was not in Jane's moribund state. For him the summer move of Miss Wardross' establishment two thousand feet up the mountain (the thinner air supposedly helping the invalids) meant a 'good-for-nothing sort of life' without the Cheltenham indolences or people to visit, though there was compensation in the beautiful, rugged and luscious landscape. Jane was pregnant.

She did not mention this in her letter to Mrs Chadwick in August. She told her of the delightful weather and the fascination of looking down upon clouds. They had not many acquaintances but she did not regret this as in the town below it was

a great bore for invalids to be dressing up and making ceremony calls, and really considering the amount of invalidism, there was a fearful amount of vanity and worldlymindedness, to say nothing of gossip, ceremony & stuckupishness. Then they had balls constantly where young men who ought to have been in their beds could not resist dancing in spite of their coughs − where sisters who had come out to nurse a dying brother would appear three days before his death- and in the spring they made up country excursions & parties of pleasure of which the doctors say openly that they cost them a certain number of patients yearly − It is also painful to see the self-deception of people about their own state or that of their friends. It is I suppose part of the complaint to be over hopeful about oneself − but it is strange to see the relations so blinded…

The two English Doctors here are considered very clever and though one sometimes hears of their being mistaken, I fancy they have as much experience of their line of cases as is possible − In the Island it is common to recommend 18 months stays but the Doctors do it with judgement knowing the effect of the heat on some constitutions − Dr Lund thinks the <u>excitement</u> of going home to England for four months very bad for some patients but no one has fathomed the extent of mischief done by the <u>dullness</u> of the summer here for those who are well − Sarah has frequently declared herself ready to "commit suicide or something worse" & David has often announced himself at the <u>lowest </u>depth when a fortnight worse than ever has revealed a "lower still" − It is rather like ship board in this − that if it were not for the meals and a good appetite to take to them it would be insupportable.[358]

Jane was still able to look about herself, and some faint, copied sketches remain among her letters. In considering the local people's houses, she was perhaps contrasting their thermal qualities with those of the iron house:

The cottages have thick stone walls, but no window – one room only – and a steep thatched roof. The cottage is generally fitted into the side of the hill so that the roof touches the ground behind and the door is in front – they look more like bee hives than houses – but in summer they are dark and cool like underground dwellings, in winter no cold can get in if the door is shut, & I suppose they resist the heavy rains.[359]

Heavily pregnant, Jane wrote to her mother-in-law in December 1860 that sturdy Charlie had 'enjoyed all the gaiety about the Empress of Austria's arrival very much'. The Empress had hired the house next door, but ' goes about dressed so plain that people hardly know her'.[360]

By the new-year, David told his mother, Jane was 'rather worn out & done up with it'.[361] Jane's last letter was in January 1861. She told her mother-in-law that they had had a dull Christmas due to her illness:

It is fortunate that we have such a good airy sitting room with two sofas and an easy chair adjoining my bed room – so that we are very comfortable ourselves and have plenty of room for any of the ladies when they come up to pay me a visit – I have had my throat in such a bad state that I could hardly speak or swallow, or lay my head on the pillow, without distress and it continued very bad for a fortnight – The doctor seems to think it arises from debility and encourages me to keep up my strength in every way…I dare say I shall not get fairly well of it till after my confinement…

[Charlie] has had several little boxes of toys given him and he plays very nicely with them sitting at my table on a chair made high with a cushion – He speaks much plainer now & begins to ask questions.[362]

Edwin Cannan, named after Edwin Chadwick who was to be his godfather, was born on February 3rd, 1861. Not quite thirty-nine, Jane died two weeks later, and was buried in Funchal's English cemetery.

Postscript

There is no record of the arrangements for Jane's funeral, nor of David's sombre return with his two little sons to England. Edwin was wet-nursed by a Portuguese woman, and was photographed with her as proxy for his mother. In Bournemouth she tried to conceal the fact that her milk had dried up. Just in time it was discovered that the tiny baby was starving.

David's sister Agnes moved in to help with the children. What must Charlie have felt as he watched her coughing death only three years later? David's sister Margaret then stepped in until David's remarriage, but is hard to imagine this as a cheerful household. He pottered around Bournemouth with cronies older than himself, became an elder and treasurer in the Scotch (Presbyterian) church, and went every day to the Reading Room on the pier approach.[363] Edwin's health being delicate, the household moved to Bristol in order that he could be a day-boy at Clifton School.

David died suddenly in a hotel in Limerick, while on a tour of western Ireland, aged only fifty-one. He had called on Webb in Dublin, now active in the Home Rule movement, who was shocked to hear of the death. Many years later Webb wrote to Charles; despite reminiscing about Jane's sketches in *The Mermaid* on board *Hempsyke*, he was disappointed to have had 'an answer dry as a bone'.[364]

The two boys became solemn, scholarly figures. Both had the university education that fate denied David, and both, cushioned by Uncle Charles' legacy, lived the rest of their lives in Oxford. Edwin, in his godfather Chadwick's footsteps, became an economist and Professor at the new, left-leaning London School of Economics.[365] He married a Scottish cousin, Rita Cullen. It was Edwin who traced his Claude and Cannan ancestry and collected together his mother's letters.

Charles Cannan, a classicist, became Dean of Trinity College, Oxford University. With a formidable manner, he put his energies into greatly expanding the scope and scale of the Oxford University Press, becoming Secretary to the Delegates from 1898 until his death in 1919.[366] He married aloof Mary Wedderburn, daughter of a wealthy Scots laird. Their three daughters Margaret Dorothea, May Wedderburn and Joanna Maxwell always considered themselves Scots, the only trace of their Claude ancestry perhaps in naming Dorothea after Jane Dorothea. Their youth was blighted by the First World War, and, like others, they may have downplayed German connections, recasting the Claudes more romantically as straightforwardly French.

The original band of Claude brothers – Adolphe, Louis and Charles – who set out from Berlin and Danzig at the end of the Napoleonic wars – left no descendants in Europe with the Claude name. There are records of descent in middle names, for instance Jane's sister Louise named her son John Claude White. Born in India, and trained as an engineer, he built roads, bridges, and railways in Bengal. He used his next positions as political agent in Sikkim and his accompaniment of Younghusband on the infamous British adventure in Tibet to explore the mountainous region of north eastern India and to discover its peoples during the late nineteenth century. He left a priceless photographic record.[367]

There are Chilean descendants. Adolphe Claude prospered through the company Schwager-Claude y Co, and had two children, Frederico Claude Schwager and Wilemmina Claude Schwager.

Jane's brother Louis remained in the USA, moving to Wisconsin during the Civil War to avoid living in a slave-owning society. He invested in land and a vineyard, and became a partner in a large water-mill which produced wooden goods and furniture.[368] He built an extraordinary gothic house on Devil's Lake. Decorated with his own carvings, it was full of curious objects and antiques, which embedded themselves in the memories of children who visited.[369] He and Elvira Ward had two children, called – naturally – Louis and

Louise. Louis Ward Claude became an innovative architect in the firm of Claude and Starck, designing many public buildings.[370] Louise, educated by her father, and with a large library, never married and devoted herself, as had her father, to the conservation of the scenery and birdlife at Eagle Crag.

The name Claude was given as a middle name by Louis' great friend, Arthur Withington, to his son Arthur Claude Withington, born in 1855. This was a mark of gratitude to Louis for getting him and his Cooper relatives over the Atlantic to what Allan Withington's wife Sarah Cooper called 'Claudeland'. Sarah's letter home conjures an Arcadian scene of young families settled within view of each other, and sharing the planting of fruit and vegetables. Though there were rattlesnakes to avoid, the homesteaders were surrounded by birds and butterflies and she and Elvira had time to sketch wildflowers, practice music and read.[371]

And what of Mary Cannan, Jane's great friend? After a stay in Florence, Mary was again a governess (unhappily) at the Laces in Yorkshire, and then to the two Miss Cloughs in Kingston. Their father Arthur Clough had died, also prematurely, in Florence very near the time of Jane's death. In old age, thanks to an annuity from W.R. Greg, Mary built herself a house in the Lake District at Grasmere, which she named the Shieling after the Cannan's ancestral Galloway property. She outlived all her siblings, dying at the age of ninety-three, remembered as a formidable old lady who kept a cow and enjoyed the river Rothay running through her garden.[372] Like her father, she was a firm Liberal, a reader of the *Manchester Guardian* and strongly believed in exercising her right to vote in local elections. The last time she did so, she was driven down to Grasmere in a motor car, but being accustomed to taking time to gaze at the Lakeland beauty, she found the experience distasteful.[373]

Mary Cannan and Mary Claude were neighbours – but were they on intimate – or indeed any – terms during their old age? Charles Cannan, an accomplished mountaineer and Alpinist, loved the Lake District and would surely have visited his bright and upright aunt Mary Cannan. The only record of any attempt to visit his other aunt

Mary is from his daughter, the poet May Cannan. She recalled an old lady in a red dressing gown. As the Charles Cannan family understood 'she rather took to the bottle', they did not go in. [374] Mary Claude, the delicate sister who had apparently needed so much from Jane, died the year after Mary Cannan, in 1912.

Of Jane's wider circle, Alfred Webb played a major role in the Irish home rule movement. He became interested in the Indian independence struggle, and in 1894 became one of the very few non-Indians to preside over the Indian National Congress. He made parallels with the Irish cause, his address bringing together the campaigns which he had fought over the past forty years: anti-slavery, temperance, franchise reform, church disestablishment. [375]

Andrew Pollock had mixed fortunes on his return to South Australia. He became Secretary at the Duryea Mining Company and was subsequently employed in the Adelaide fire office under his old friend Edmund Wright. Known as a sober and honourable family man (he had married in 1859) his suicide in 1864 caused consternation in the community. His final letter to Wright, from whom he had tried to conceal his borrowing of £200 from the fire office, suggested that grave financial problems had led him to imagine that the only way out was for his family to receive his life insurance. The papers remarked that the failure of Morewood & Rogers had reduced his circumstances very much. [376] Something positive came out of this story. Pollock's daughter Gertrude married Alfred Wells, an architect, and their descendents continue to live in South Australia.

What of the firm whose patent galvanising processes touched all these people? George Rogers died in 1861, having been an invalid for several years. Edmund Morewood never married, being perhaps married to the firm which rose again, phoenix-like, when he went into partnership with Rogers' son, John Henry Rogers. These two established the South Wales Tinplate Co at Machynys with five mills on the back of Morewood & Co's iron works in Birmingham and South Wales. By the 1880s the firm had become the fourth largest in the world for tinplate production, with thirteen workshops at Llanelli and seven at Swansea. Morewood died in 1887. [377]

★

Let's imagine Mary Cannan's contentment in her house in Grasmere, which like the fruitful homestead of Louis and the Withingtons is surely what Jane would have wanted. She and her three children in the little iron house in Melbourne, perhaps graduating to a wooden house with a shady, flower-laden veranda surrounded by trees, reading, teaching, talking with congenial company, and suspended above insecurity by Uncle Charles. She would have applauded Annie Clough's achievement in becoming the first principal of Cambridge University's Newnham College in 1871. Augusta Wotherspoon's daughter was among her first students and Jane would have wished (remembering those closed doors at the lecture-halls in Berlin) that her Louisa might have joined this little group of pioneering women.[378] Above all, she would have been under an umbrella, as her cousin Adolphe remembered her, sketching buildings, scenery, and mothers and children among goats and washing lines.[379]

Jane's granddaughter Joanna Cannan, a writer and novelist, imagined the adventurous Jane resisting leaving Australia with David, refusing the prospect of pleasant, dull England with its tedious embroidering of antimacassars and presiding over tea pots. As David sleeps and dreams of percentages and investments, Jane makes off at dawn with the vigorous Archie Cullen. 'Could you sleep under the stars with a horse-rug for a blanket and your saddle for a pillow?' Archie asks her. 'Sounder than in the best Lake District bedroom,' she replies, planning to cut her hair and buy britches to ride astride Red Dawn. Off they ride, to a place he's discovered where they will build a cabin and stake their boundaries.[380] I think, though, that she had hoped to do this with David – but fate was against both of them.

Notes

Abbreviations

Jane Cannan: JDC
David Cannan: DAC
National Library of Australia: NLA. The Jane and David Cannan correspondence
    they hold is referred to in the notes as 401.
Trinity College, University of Oxford: Their Cannan papers are referred to in the
    notes as DD262.
Harry Ransom Humanities Research Centre (Hartley Coleridge correspondence): HRC.

Introduction

1   Both quotes JDC to Mary Cannan, 16 July 1852. DD262/K8.

2   Harriet Martineau to Jane Claude, 2 August 1852, in LSE letter collection, and in Logan, *The Collected Letters of Harriet Martineau*, vol 3, pp. 240-1.

3   Hartley Coleridge to Mrs Henry Nelson Coleridge, April 10 1847, in Griggs and Griggs *Letters of Hartley Coleridge*, letter 91.

4   B.A. Clough, *A Memoir of Anne Jemima Clough*, Annie Clough, *Notebook 10*, 1847.

5   National Trust of Australia (Victoria): Portable Iron Houses at 399 Coventry Street, South Melbourne. Pieper: 'Portable Iron Houses', pp. 28-31.

6   Evans and Lycett Green, *English Cottages*. Lyall, *Dream Cottages – from Cottage Ornée to Stockbroker Tudor*. Herbert, *Pioneers of Prefabrication – the British contribution in the Nineteenth Century*, p.3.

7   Hassam, *Sailing to Australia – shipboard diaries by nineteenth century British emigrants*, pp. 26-40.

8   Thomson and Banfill 'Corrugated-Iron Buildings: an endangered resource within the built heritage', pp. 71-72.

9   See for instance Reeder, *The Vision Splendid*, pp. 96-101. Kerr, *Dictionary of Australian Artists*, entry for Jane Cannan. Terry, *Cooee: Australia in the 19th century*, p. 44. Lewis, 'Notes on Jane Cannan's Drawings' .

10   Jordan, *Picturesque Pursuits – colonial women artists & the amateur tradition*.
11   Lewis, 'Notes on Jane Cannan's Drawings'.
12   Rita Cannan: 'In Memoriam: Mary Louisa Cannan, an old Gallovidian'.

Chapter One: A Huguenot Childhood: Liverpool

13   David Cannan to Mrs Cannan 15 August. 401(4).
14   JDC to Mrs Cannan 15 August 1853. 401(4).
15   Hassam, *Sailing to Australia – shipboard diaries by nineteenth century British emigrants*, p. 204.
16   Louis Claude to his sister Louise Claude, 16 April 1817. DD262addB/2.
17   Gore's Directory, 1825.
18   Aughton, *Liverpool – A People's History*, pp. 124-5.
19   Marriner, *Rathbones of Liverpool, 1845-73*. Simey, *Charitable Effort in Liverpool in the Nineteenth Century*.
20   Williams, 'Liverpool Merchants and the Cotton Trade 1820-1850'.
21   Mendez Baltrán, *La Exportacion Minera en Chile 1800-1840*. Tayleur is also spelt Tailleur in this book, according to which the company was the forth largest exporter of gold in the period 1800-1840.
22   *London Gazette*, 6 April 1822, Issue 17806, p. 589.
23   Mrs Louise Claude to her aunt Dorothea Pfeffer, 29 January 1826. In author's possession.
24   'Marvellously odd' was Southey's description (see Gee, *Bricks without Mortar: the selected poems of Hartley Coleridge)*. Letter to Mrs Samuel Taylor Coleridge, May 16 1835, in Griggs and Griggs, *Letters of Hartley Coleridge*, letter 49.
25   Hartley Coleridge to Mrs S.T.Coleridge, 6 November, 1836, in Griggs and Griggs, letter 57.
26   Hartley Coleridge to Mrs Samuel Taylor Coleridge, October 28, 1836, in Griggs and Griggs, letter 56.
27   Mrs Claude to Hartley Coleridge, ?late 1840, HRC.
28   Hartley Coleridge to Mrs Claude, September 1838, HRC.
29   JDC to Mary Cannan, 17 October 1853. 401(9).
30   JDC to Mary Cannan 22 February 1852. DD262/K8.
31   Mary Claude to Hartley Coleridge, no date (?late 1838) HRC.
32   Gwynne, *Huguenot Heritage*.
33   Mrs Claude to Dorothea Pfeffer, 29 January 1826. In author's possession.
34   Flanders, *The Victorian House – domestic life from childbirth to deathbed*, pp. 48-62.
35   Mrs Claude to Hartley Coleridge, no date, c 1838/9. HRC.
36   Mrs Claude to Hartley Coleridge ?late 1840. HRC.
37   Harriet Martineau's *A Year at Ambleside*, in Todd, *Harriet Martineau at Ambleside*, p. 85.
38   Mrs Claude to Hartley Coleridge, ?late 1840. HRC.

39   Mrs Claude to Hartley Coleridge, c autumn 1840. HRC.
40   Mrs Claude to Hartley Coleridge, 18 April 1841; 7 November, 1841; JDC
      to Hartley Coleridge, 12 December 1841. All HRC.
41   JDC to Mary Cannan, 22nd November 1852. DD262, K6, K14 and K8.
42   Pattinson, *The Great Age of Steam on Windermere*, pp27-30.
43   Mrs Claude to Hartley Coleridge, 15 March 1847, HRC.

Chapter Two: A somewhat Amazonian society: Ambleside and the Lake District

44   Todd, *Harriet Martineau at Ambleside*, pp. 54-5.
45   JDC to Mary Cannan 16 July 1852. DD262/K8. Anne Clough *Notebook 10*,
      June 1847. Mary Claude, *Natural History in Stories*.
46   Mary Claude to Hartley Coleridge, undated ?1838, HRC.
47   Kenny, *Arthur Hugh Clough, A Poet's Life*, pp. 105-6.
48   Honan, *Matthew Arnold, A Life*, pp. 155-6.
49   Murray, *A Life of Matthew Arnold*. Cited in *Oxford Dictionary of National
      Biography* Matthew Arnold entry by Collini. Honan, *Matthew Arnold*, Chapter
      7. Bertram (ed), *The New Zealand Letters of Tom Arnold*; it is Tom Arnold's letter
      of June 14 1849 (letter 37) that refers to the Arnold mirth over Matthew
      Arnold's romantic passion for Mary Claude.
50   JDC to Mary Cannan, 16 July 1852. DD262/K8.
51   JDC to Jeannette ?autumn 1852. DD262/K6.
52   Margaret and Agnes Cannan to Mary Cannan, April 20 1853. DD262/addB/3.
53   Kenny, *Arthur Hugh Clough*, pp. 109-110 and 77.
54   Kaplan, 'Thomas Carlyle', in *Dictionary of National Biography*. On Clough and
      Carlyle as 'somewhat heathenish' – see Kenny, *Arthur Hugh Clough*, p. 52.
55   Clough, B.A. *A Memoir of Anne Jemima Clough*, p.67.
56   JDC to Mary Cannan 16 July 1852. DD262/K8.
57   Todd, *Harriet Martineau at Ambleside*, pp.52-3.
58   Peterson, *Autobiography – Harriet Martineau*, pp. 539-544.
59   Peterson, *Autobiography – Harriet Martineau*, p. 310.
60   Todd, *Harriet Martineau at Ambleside*, pp. 133-4
61   JDC to Mary Cannan, 22 November 1852. DD262/K6, K14, K8.
62   Todd, *Harriet Martineau at Ambleside*, pp.168-9.
63   Peterson , *Autobiography – Harriet Martineau*, p. 285.
64   Harriet Martineau to JDC, August 21 ?1852, LSE letter collection.
65   JDC to Mary Cannan, 28 October, ?1852, DD262 Edwin Cannan Transcript.
66   JDC to Mary Cannan, 22 November 1852. DD262/K6, 14, 8.
67   Sutherland, *Faith, Duty and the Power of Mind – the Cloughs and their circle
      1820-1860*. Chapter 3. Much of Annie Clough's journal (Notebook 10 at
      Newnham College University of Cambridge) is included in B.A.Clough's
      A Memoir of Anne Jemima Clough.

68   Clough, B.A. *A Memoir of Anne Jemima Clough*, Chapter IV.
69   Sutherland, *Faith, Duty and the Power of Mind*, p. 46; Thompson, *The Rise of Respectable Society – a social history of Victorian Britain*, pp.142-50.
70   JDC to Mary Cannan, 22 February 1852. DD262/K8.
71   Clough, B.A., *A Memoir of Anne Jemima Clough*, pp. 66 and 82.
72   JDC to Mary Cannan, 16 July 1852. DD262/K8.
73   JDC to Jeannette Claude, 25 October 1850. DD262/K25.
74   JDC ?to Jeannette Claude, undated. DD262/K6.
75   Barringer, 'The last of England', p.32.
76   Heaseman, *Evangelicals in Action,* Chapter V.
77   Clough, B.A. A *Memoir of Anne Jemima.Clough*, p.62.
78   Armstrong, *The English Parson-Naturalist*, p.53. And Moss, *A Bird in the Bush – a social history of birdwatching*, p. 46.
79   JDC to Jeannette Claude, undated. DD262/K6.
80   JDC to Jeannette Claude, 22 October 1850. DD262/K6.
81   Briggs, *Victorian People*, Chapter 2. Thompson, *The Rise of Respectable Society – a social history of Victorian Britain*, p. 38.
82   Herbert, *Pioneers of Prefabrication – the British contribution in the Nineteenth Century*, pp. 1-2.
83   *Catalogue of the Great Exhibition.* Classes I and IX. 1851.
84   *Catalogue of the Great Exhibition*, Class VII.
85   Briggs, *Iron Bridge to Crystal Palace*, p.171.
86   Journals of Louis J. Claude, Sauk County Historical Society, Baraboo, Wisconsin.
87   JDC to Mary Cannan 20 and 22 December 1851. DD262 Edwin Cannan's transcript and K27.
88   JDC to Mary Cannan, 28 October 1852. DD262 Edwin Cannan's transcript.
89   JDC to Mary Cannan, 22 November 1852. DD262/K6, K14, K8.
90   JDC to Mary Cannan, 16 July 1852. DD262/K8.
91   JDC to Mary Cannan, 28 October 1852. DD262 Edwin Cannan's transcript.
92   JDC to Mary Cannan, 28 October, 1852. DD262 Edwin Cannan's transcript.
93   JDC to Mary Cannan, 22 February 1852. DD262/K8.
94   JDC to Mary Cannan, 27 September 1853, 401(8).
95   JDC to Jeannette Claude, ?autumn 1852. DD262/K6.
96   JDC to Mary Cannan, 16 July 1852. DD262/K8.
97   JDC to Mary Cannan, 22 November 1852. DD262/K6, K14, K8.

Chapter Three: A timid kiss and talk of corrugated iron

98   Lewis, 'The Epigraphy of the Iron Tile'; Thomson, and Banfill, 'Corrugated-Iron Buildings: an endangered resource within the built heritage', Herbert, *Pioneers of Prefabrication – the British Contribution in the nineteenth century*, pp. 67-74. Llanelli History website: Edmund Morewood & John Rogers. An 1854 Trade Directory gives their Birmingham office as 11 Broad Street, Easy Row.

99   Pollock correspondence and notebook.
100   John Jones (1821) an operative spinner at M'Connel and Kennedy, quoted in Lee, *A Cotton Enterprise 1795-1840: a history of M'Connel & Kennedy, fine cotton spinners*, p. 1. Also in Briggs, A, *Iron Bridge to Crystal Palace*, p. 67. Briggs has 'nurse' for muse – somewhat less poetic. DNB entry for John Kennedy also by Lee.
101   Cannan, *In Memorian: Mary Louisa Cannan, an old Gallovidian.*
102   Howe, *The Cotton Masters 1830-1860*, pp. 70-77 and 270ff. Briggs, *Victorian Cities,* chapter III.
103   Edwin Cannan's notes, DD262, Add/B13.
104   McConnel & Co, 9 September 1851, UCL Chadwick Archive 435.
105   David Cannan to Mary Cannan, 14 March 1855. DD262/K29. David Cannan's son Edwin Cannan's unpublished account tells of the Chadwick position.
106   Ackroyd, *Dickens*, pp. 382-5. Ackroyd, *London – the biography*, pp. 541-543, 574-5, and 431-437.
107   JDC to Mary Cannan, 20 December 1851. DD262/K27.
108   JDC to Mary Cannan, 22 February 1852. DD262/K8.
109   Farr, *Gilbert Cannan – a Georgian Prodigy.* The writer Gilbert Cannan was James' grandson.
110   Gwynne, *Huguenot Heritage*, pp. 4-15. And cf the life and writing of Samuel Smiles.
111   JDC to Jeannette Claude, undated. DD262/K6.
112   JDC to Jeannette Claude, undated. DD262/K6.
113   JDC to Mary Cannan, 22 November. DD262/K6, 14, 8.
114   Peterson, (ed) *Autobiography – Harriet Martineau*, pp. 612-613.
115   JDC to Emil du Bois Raymond,? January 1853. DD262/K6.
116   Louis Claude journal, August 1852. Sauk County Historical Society.
117   JDC to Mary Cannan, 16 July 1852. DD262/K8.
118   Finer, *The Life and Times of Sir Edwin Chadwick*, p. 5.
119   JDC to Jeannette Claude, autumn 1852. DD262/K8.
120   JDC to Jeannette, undated DD262/K6.
121   JDC to Jeannette Claude, autumn 1852. DD262/K8.
122   JDC to Jeannette, undated. DD262/K6.
123   JDC to Mary Cannan, 17 January 1853. DD262/K29.
124   JDC to Jeannette Claude, undated. DD262/K6.
125   JDC to Mary Cannan, 17 January 1853. DD262/K29.
126   Ibid.

Chapter Four: Radiantly happy and many weeping goodbyes

127   *The Edinburgh Courant*, 'Portable Metallic Houses for Australia' 1 April 1853.
128   Keneally, *The Commonwealth of Thieves – the story of the founding of Australia*, pp. 165 and 279.

129   Herbert, *Pioneers of Prefabrication – the British contribution in the nineteenth century*, pp. 4ff, and 61-74.

130   *Bristol Mercury*, 16 October 1852.

131   Bristol Reference Library, Clift House collection, newspaper cutting undated.

132   For instance in *The Times* 4 March 1853.

133   *Illustrated London News*, February 18 1854.

134   Pollock Transcribed Notebook 1, 10 November 1851.

135   Hughes, *The Short Life and Long Times of Mrs Beeton*, pp. 147, 149 and 229.

136   JDC to Jeannette Claude, ? February 1853. DD262/K6.

137   David Cannan to Mary Cannan, March 14 1853. DD262/K29.

138   JDC to Jeannette Claude, no date. DD262/K6.

139   JDC to Agnes Cannan, undated, ? March 1853. DD262/K6.

140   Harriet Martineau to Mary Carpenter, in Logan (ed) vol 3, 247. Logan gives the date as November 1852, but it must have been April 1853.

141   Harriet Martineau to Richard Webb, 1 May 1853, in Logan ed, vol 3, 277-8. And Legg: *Alfred Webb, the autobiography of a Quaker Nationalist*, Introduction.

142   Harriet Martineau to David Cannan, 1st May 1853. DD262/K19.

143   Thompson, *The Rise of Respectable Society – a social history of Victorian Britain*, Chapter 3. Jane's settlement is in DD262/Add/A1.

144   Charles Claude to JDC, December 30 1853. DD262/AddB/5.

145   Margaret and Agnes Cannan to Mary Cannan, April 20 1853. DD262/add/B/3; they copied the note quoted below from David to his mother.

146   *Ibid.*

147   JDC to Mrs Cannan, May 1853. DD262/K29.

148   JDC to Jeannette Claude, undated. DD262/K6.

149   JDC to Jeannette Claude, undated. DD262/K6.

150   Harriet Martineau to Richard Webb, 1 May 1853, in Logan ed, vol 3, 277-8.

151   Pollock: *Observations of an Early Colonist*, pp. 37-39.

152   Charles Dickens in *Household Words*, 17 July 1852. Quoted in Serle, *The Golden Age, A History of the Colony of Victoria*, p. 38.

153   *The Times*, 9 April, 1853.

154   Greenhill. and Giffard, *Travelling by Sea in the Nineteenth Century – interior design in Victorian passenger ships*, Chapter 2. And see Terry, 'The Voyage' in Macdonald (ed), *Epic Journeys in the Victorian Era*.

155   JDC to Agnes Cannan, 5 May 1853. 401(2).

156   JDC to Mrs Cannan, 5 May 1853. 401(1).

157   JDC to Jeannette Claude, undated but contents indicate 6 May 1853. DD262/K6.

158   Charles Dickens, *David Copperfield*, originally published in 1849-50. Collins edition, p. 811. And see Hassam, *Sailing to Australia*, who contrasts the confusion with attempts to make cabins cosy and home-like.

159   JDC to Jeannette Claude, undated. DD262/K6.

Chapter Five: The floating home: Hempsyke

160 Webb, *Autobiography*, pp.197 -199.
161 JDC to Jeannette Claude/du Bois Raymond, 2 June 1853, 401(3). According to the passenger list, the doctor is Edward or Edwin Hall, but no age is given (Victoria PRO – Unassisted Immigration to Victoria).
162 Webb, *Autobiography*, p. 199.
163 Pollock, '*Observations of an early Colonist*, pp. 10-11.
164 Woolcock, *Rites of Passage – emigration to Australia in the nineteenth century*, pp. 114-137. Terry, 'The Voyage'.
165 According to the passenger list in the Victoria PRO, John Campbell and his wife were 28 and 25.
166 JDC to Jeannette Claude/du Bois Raymond, 7 August, 1853, 401(3).
167 Thomas Goldsmith, 27 (passenger list). Many of the ages on the passenger list appear inaccurate – as are Jane Cannan's and Webb's, so we must be cautious about this information.
168 Mr Grote on the passenger list, John Germans Grote on the testimonial list, Rootsweb Aussie archives. He may be the nephew of the classical historian, radical politician, member of the Council of University College of London, and financial supporter of the *Westminster Review*, George Grote 1794-1871. See Ashton, *142 Strand*.
169 George Watson, 30, on the passenger list.
170 JDC to Jeannette Claude/du Bois Raymond, undated, DD262/K6.
171 Hassam, *Sailing to Australia: shipboard diaries by nineteenth century emigrants*, p. 116.
172 Pollock, '*Observations of an early Colonist*', pp. 8-11.
173 Edgar Baker, 28, is the only Baker listed.
174 JDC to Jeannette Claude/du Bois Raymond, 2 June 1853, 401(3).
175 JDC to Jeannette Claude/du Bois Raymond, undated. DD262/K6.
176 JDC to Jeannette Claude/du Bois Raymond, 2 June 1853. 401(3).
177 Webb, *Autobiography,* pp. 200-1 and p. 239.
178 Woolcock, *Rites of Passage – emigration to Australia in the nineteenth century*, pp. 147-8.
179 JDC to Jeannette Claude/du Bois Raymond, 401(3) iii of iii.
180 JDC to Jeannette Claude/du Bois Raymond, 14 August 1853. 401(3).
181 JDC to Mary Cannan, 27 September 1853. 401(8).
182 JDC to Jeannette Claude/du Bois Raymond, 7 August 1853. 401(3).
183 JDC to Jeannette Claude/du Bois Raymond, 1 July 1853. DD262/K6.
184 JDC to Jeannette Claude/du Bois Raymond, 7 August 1853. 401(3) ii of iii.
185 JDC to Jeannette Claude/du Bois Raymond, 1 July 1853. DD262/K6.
186 David Cannan to Mrs Cannan, 9 July 1853. 401(4).
187 JDC to Jeannette Claude/du Bois Raymond, 1 July 1853. DD262/K6.
188 David Cannan to Mrs Cannan, 3 July 1853. 401(4).
189 JDC to Jeannette Claude/du Bois Raymond, 1 July 1853. DD262/K6.

190   JDC to Jeannette Claude/du Bois Raymond, 1 July 1853. DD262/K6.

191   JDC to Jeannette Claude/du Bois Raymond, 1 July 1853. DD262/K6.

192   JDC to Jeannette Claude/du Bois Raymond, 7 August, 1853. 401(3).

193   JDC to Jeannette Claude/du Bois Raymond, 7 August 1853. 401(3).

194   Webb, *Autobiography*, p. 203.

195   David Cannan to Mrs Cannan, 3 July, 1853. 401(4).

196   Hammerton, *Emigrant Gentlewomen, genteel poverty and female emigration 1830-1914*, Chapter 4. Serle, *The Golden Age, A history of the colony of Victoria*, p.55. Casteras, 'Women and children last'.

197   JDC to Jeannette Claude/du Bois Raymond, 2 June 1853. 401(3) i of iii.

198   Hassam, *Sailing to Australia – shipboard diaries by nineteenth century British emigrants*, p. 69.

199   JDC to Jeannette Claude/du Bois Raymond, 7 August 1853. 401(3).

200   JDC to Jeannette Claude/du Bois Raymond, 2 June 1853. 401(3).

201   Greenhill, and Giffard, *Travelling by Sea in the Nineteenth Century – interior design in Victorian passenger ships*, Chapter 2. Terry, 'The Voyage'.

202   JDC to Jeannette Claude/du Bois Raymond, 7 August 1853. 401(3).

203   Webb, *Autobiography,* p. 203.

204   David Cannan to Mrs Cannan, 11 August, 1853. 401(4).

205   JDC to Jeannette Claude/du Bois Raymond, 14 August 1853. 401(3). In the end 51 passengers signed – the Cannans and Webb not among them, though Mr Ordish, Mr Campbell, Mr Grote, and Mr Hall were. www.rootsweb.com/aussie-gen-research-L-Hempsyke.

206   JDC to Jeannette Claude/du Bois Raymond, 14 August 1853. 401 (3).

207   JDC to Jeannette Claude/du Bois Raymond, 14 August 1853. 401(3).

208   JDC to Jeannette Claude/du Bois Raymond, 7 August 1853. 401(3).

209   JDC to Jeannette du Bois Raymond, 22 September 1854. 401(14).

Chapter Six: Totally unfit for genteel people: Melbourne

210   Immigrant quoted in Serle, *The Golden Age*, p. 92.

211   Briggs, Victorian Cities, p. 51.

212   David Cannan wrote that Melbourne was 'totally unfit for genteel people' to Hannah Greg, 22 January, 1854. 401(11).

213   Webb, *Autobiograph,y* pp. 204-212.

214   Young American Abroad – quoted in Serle, *The Golden Age*, p.121.

215   Keneally, *The Commonwealth of Thieves*, p.275, and Serle, *The Golden Age*, pp. 47-51.

216   Pollock correspondence.

217   JDC to James Cannan 24 August 1853. 401(5).

218   JDC to Mary Cannan, 11 September 1853. 401(6).

219   Pollock, *Observations*, pp. 55-62.

220   JDC to her aunt (Jeanette's mother), 21 September 1853. 401(7B).

221   JDC to Mary Cannan, 11 September 1853. 401(6).
222   JDC to her aunt (Jeannette's mother), 21 September 1853. 401 (7B).
223   JDC to her aunt (Jeannette's mother) 21 September 1853, 401(7B).
224   Annear, *Bearbrass – Imagining Early Melbourne*.
225   Rayment, MS diary quoted by Serle, *The Golden Age*, p. 68.
226   Pollock, *Observations*, p. 43.
227   *Argus*, 11 Dec 1852, letters.
228   Pollock to Isabelle Pollock, 13 January 1851.
229   JDC to Mary Cannan, 27 September 1853. 401(8).
230   Pollock to Morewood & Rogers 22 December 1850; *South Australian Register*, 16 May 1851.
231   Pollock, *Observations*, p. 41.
232   Lewis 'Notes on Jane Dorothea Cannan's drawings' p.70. Letter John Tregenza to Eleanor Wells 5 August 1996.
233   Letter from Pollock to Morewood & Rogers, 22 December 1850.
234   Pollock correspondence, 22 December 1850 to Morewood & Rogers and 25 October 1851 to Union Bank, Adelaide.
235   *Argus*, 19 November 1852.
236   Lewis, 'Notes on Jane Dorothea Cannan's Drawings', p. 64. And Moore, 'Two Views from Mr Pollock's Window'.
237   David Cannan to James Cannan 24 August 1853, 401(5).
238   Lewis, 'Notes on Jane Dorothea Cannan's Drawings', p. 69.
239   JDC to James Cannan, 24 August 1853. 401(5).
240   Serle, *The Golden Age*, pp.53-6.
241   JDC to Mary Cannan, 11 September 1853, 401(4). Jane and David were right to urge caution to Mary Cannan – see Hammerton, *Emigrant Gentlewomen*.
242   JDC to Jeannette du Bois Raymond, 21 September 1853. 401(7A).
243   Louis Claude's journal, Sauk County Historical Society, Wisconsin.
244   Gaskell, *North and South*, p. 110.
245   Serle, *The Golden Age*, Chapters 3 and 5.
246   Pollock to Morewood & Rogers, 16 January 1851.
247   Pollock to Isabella Pollock, 16 January 1851.
248   JDC to Mary Cannan, 11 September 1853. 401(6).
249   JDC to her aunt (Jeannette's mother), 21 September 1853. 401(7B).
250   JDC to Jeannette, 21 September 1853. 401(7A).
251   JDC to James Cannan, 24 August 1853. 401(5).
252   JDC to Mary Cannan, 17 October 1853. 401(9).
253   JDC to Mary Cannan, 11 September 1853. 401(6).
254   JDC to Jeannette du Bois Raymond, 21 September 1853. 401(7A).
255   JDC to Jeannette Claude/du Bois Raymond, 27 November 1853. 401(10).
256   Briggs, *Victorian Cities*, pp.290-291.
257   David Cannan to Hannah Greg, 22 January 1854. 401(11).
258   JDC to Jeannette du Bois Raymond, 21 September 1853. 401(7A).

259 *Argus*, 4 June 1853.
260 JDC to Jeannette Claude/du Bois Raymond, 21 September 1853. 401(7A).
261 JDC to Jeannette du Bois Raymond, 21 September 1853. 401(7A).
262 JDC to Jeannette, 27 November 1853. 401(10).
263 JDC to Mary Cannan, 17 October 1853. 401(9).
264 David Cannan to James Cannan, 24 August 1853. 401(5).
265 David Cannan to Mary Cannan, 17 October 1853. 401(9), and David Cannan to Hannah Greg, 22 January, 1854. 401(11).
266 JDC to Mary Cannan, 17 October 1853. 401(9).

Chapter Seven: The iron house

267 DAC in JDC to Mary Cannan 11 September 1853, 401(6).
268 JDC to Mrs Cannan, 18 March 1855, 401(15).
269 Serle, *The Golden Age*, p. 3.
270 Briggs, *Victorian Cities*, pp. 288-9.
271 JDC with DAC to James Cannan, 24 August 1853, 401(5). And see Lewis, 'Notes on Jane Cannan's drawings'.
272 JDC to Jeannette Claude/du Bois Raymond, 21 September 1853, 401(7A).
273 JDC to Jeannette Claude/du Bois Raymond, 27 November 1853, 401(10).
274 JDC to Mary Cannan, 11 September 1853, 401(6).
275 JDC to Jeannette Claude/du Bois Raymond, 26 March 1854, DD262/ K6.
276 JDC to Mary Cannan, 27 September 1853. 401(8).
277 JDC to Mary Cannan, 27 September 1853, 401(8).
278 Flanders, *The Victorian House*, Introduction.
279 JDC to Mrs Cannan, 7 July 1856, 401(19).
280 Herbert, *Pioneers of Prefabrication,* pp. 47-67.
281 National Trust of Australia (Victoria), Portable Iron Houses, 399 Coventry Street, Melbourne.
282 JDC to Jeannette Claude/du Bois Raymond, 27 November 1853, 401(10).
283 JDC and DAC to Mary Cannan, 20 May 1854, 401(12).
284 JDC to Jeannette Claude/du Bois Raymond, 26 March 1854, DD262/K6.
285 JDC to Jeannette Claude/ du Bois Raymond, 27 November 1853, 401(10).
286 DAC to Hannah Greg, 22 January 1854, 401(11).
287 JDC to Agnes Cannan, 19 July 1854, 401(13).
288 JDC to Jeannette Claude/du Bois Raymond, 26 March 1854, DD262/K6.
289 Todd, *Harriet Martineau at Ambleside*, pp. 169-170.
290 JDC to Jeannette Claude/du Bois Raymond, 27 November 1853, 401 (10).
291 JDC to Mary Cannan, 27 September 1853, 401(8).
292 JDC to her aunt 21 September 1853, 401(7B).
293 JDC to Jeannette Claude/du Bois Raymond, 26 March 1854, DD262/K6.

294 JDC to Mary Cannan, 27 September 1853. 401(8).
295 Hughes, *The Short Life and Long Times of Mrs Beeton*, p. 247. Flanders, *The Victorian House,* pp. 93-4.
296 JDC and DAC to Mary Cannan, 20 May 1854, 401(12).
297 JDC to Jeannette Claude/du Bois Raymond, 21 September 1853, 401(7A).
298 JDC to Jeannette Claude/du Bois Raymond, 26 March 1854, DD262/K6.
299 JDC to Agnes Cannan, 19 July 1854, 401(13). Flanders, *The Victorian House*, p. 277ff on making calls.
300 JDC to Agnes Cannan, 19 July 1854, 401(13).
301 JDC to her aunt (Jeannette's mother), 21 September 1853. 401(7B).
302 JDC to Mary Cannan, 17 October 1853. 401(9).
303 Louis Claude's journal, Sauk County Historical Society, Wisconsin.
304 JDC to Mary Cannan, 17 October 1853, 401(9).
305 JDC to Mary Cannan, 27 September 1853, 401(8).
306 JDC to Agnes Cannan, 19 July 1854, 401(13).
307 JDC to Mary Cannan, 26 May 1854, 401(12). According to Harriet Martineau, Jane Arrowsmith was cook to the High Sheriff of Melbourne, Alistair/ Alexander McKenzie. Peterson, *Autobiography – Harriet Martineau*, p.505.
308 JDC to Jeannette Claude/du Bois Raymond, 26 March 1854, DD262/K6.
309 JDC to Jeannette Claude/du Bois Raymond 22 September 1854, 401(14).

Chapter Eight: Heavy failure in the iron trade

310 JDC to Mrs Cannan, 18 March 1855. 401(15).
311 *Argus*, 22 March 1855.
312 *Sydney Morning Herald*, 3 June 1856, and *Argus*, 31 May 1856.
313 Herbert, *Pioneers of Prefabrication*, pp. 60-68.
314 John Walker to David Cannan, 3 August 1855, DD262/K15. John Walker was probably the proprietor of the Gospel Oak sheet mill at Tipton in Staffordshire which manufactured Morewood & Rogers tiles. See Lewis, 'The Epigraphy of the Iron Tile'. Or is it possible that it is the John Walker who was a successful rival to Morewood and Rogers, based in Millwall in London (the letters to David Cannan are addressed from the City of London)? See also Herbert, *Pioneers of Prefabrication*, pp. 46-7.
315 *Colonial Times,* syndicated from the *Melbourne Morning Herald*, Hobart, 8 May 1855, and *South Australia Register*, 27 February 1855.
316 Herbert, *Pioneers of Prefabrication*, pp.67-69; Johnston, ' The Tin Tradition'. Evans, *The Australian Home*, pp. 38-39.
317 R. Adolphe Claude to JDC, 3 July 1854. DD262/add/B5. All correspondence from R. Adolphe Claude is taken from this section of the archive.
318 RAC to JDC, 12 December 1853.
319 Will of Charles Guillaume Claude. DD262/addA/2.
320 JDC to Mrs Cannan, 7 July 1856. 401(19).

321 David Cannan to Jeannette Claude/ du Bois Raymond, date not clear. 401(17).
322 JDC to Agnes Cannan, 9 May 1855. 401(16).
323 David Cannan to Mrs Cannan, 29 November 1855. 401(18).
324 JDC, presumably to Mrs Claude, letter is copied by Mrs Claude. DD262/ K15.
325 JDC to Mrs Cannan, 7 July 1856. 401(19).
326 JDC to Tom Cannan, 10 September 1856. 401(20).
327 JDC to Mrs Cannan, 7 July 1856. 401(19).
328 Webb, *Autobiography*, p. 216.
329 Pollock to his mother, 11 February 1851, and to his brother William, Easter Sunday 1851.
330 David Cannan to Mrs Cannan, 5 October 1856. 401(21).
331 Fragment of a letter from JDC, no date or addressee. DD262/K6.

Chapter Nine: Smoothing the descent to the grave: Madeira

332 Dubos, *The White Plague,* Chapter VI and p. 101. Smith, *The Retreat of TB*, p. 134.
333 Dyster, 'Madeira as a Residence for Invalids', pp. 943-944.
334 Camara, 'The Image and Tourism Industry of Madeira 1850-1914'.
335 JDC to Mrs Cannan, 17 July 1857, DD262/K16.
336 JDC to Jeannette Claude, 20 July 1857, DD262/K16.
337 JDC to David Cannan October 22 1857, DD262/K16.
338 JDC to DAC, October 22 1857, DD262/K16, and JDC to Mrs Cannan, 17 July 1857, DD262/K16.
339 Briggs, *Victorian Cities*, pp. 133-4.
340 JDC to Mrs Cannan, 17 July 1857, DD262/K16.
341 JDC to Mrs Cannan, 24 December 1858, DD262/K17.
342 JDC to Jeannette du Bois Raymond, 20 July 1857, DD262/K16.
343 JDC to Jeannette du Bois Raymond, 2 January 1860, DD262/K21.
344 Probably Agnes (Mrs James) Cannan to possibly Rita (Mrs Edwin) Cannan, April 29, no year. DD262 K6.
345 R. Adolphe Claude to JDC 29 June 1858. All the Adolphe Claude letters are in DD262/add/B5.
346 30 October 1859.
347 JDC to Agnes Cannan, 1 September 1858, DD262/K17.
348 David Cannan to JDC, guesswork makes it autumn 1858, DD262/K17.
349 JDC to Agnes Cannan, 12 May, 1859, DD262/K18.
350 JDC to Jeannette du Bois Raymond, 7 July 1859, DD262/K18.
351 JDC to Jeannette du Bois Raymond, 29 October 1859, DD262/K18.
352 JDC to Jeannette du Bois Raymond, 29 October 1859, DD262/K18.
353 JDC to Mrs Cannan, 5 November 1859, DD262/K18.

354 David Cannan to Mrs Cannan, 28 November 1859, DD262/K21.
355 JDC to Mrs Cannan, January 1860, DD262/K21.
356 JDC to Jeannette du Bois Raymond, 2 January 1860, DD262/K21.
357 These details taken from letters all in DD262/K21 in 1860 to Mrs Cannan and Jeannette.
358 JDC to Mrs Chadwick, 27 August 1860, DD262/K30.
359 JDC to Mrs Chadwick, 27 August 1860, DD262/K30.
360 JDC to Mrs Cannan, 4 December 1860, DD262/K21.
361 DAC to Mrs Cannan, 2 January 1861, DD262/K21.
362 JDC to Mrs Cannan, 8 January 1861, DD262/K21. Jane mistakenly dated it 1860.

Postscript

363 Edwin Cannan's notes on David Alexander Cannan. DD262/addB13.
364 Webb, *Autobiography*, p. 200. Letter Webb to Edwin Cannan, 17 October 1903, DD262/K7.
365 Cannan, E., 'Pages from an Autobiography'; Gregory, 'Edwin Cannan: a personal impression'.
366 Maw, 'Charles Cannan' in *Oxford Dictionary of National Biography*, 2004.
367 Meyer, *In the Shadow of the Himalayas – a photographic record by John Claude White 1883-1908*.
368 Obituary in *The Baraboo Republic*, June 29th 1893; See *Sketches of Sauk County* by William H. Canfield, Baraboo, A.N. Kellog, 1861, pp.12-13, in the Sauk County Historical Museum.
369 See letter from William G.Evenson to Mrs Rita Cannan, 31st July 1954 (author's possession) and letter from Margaret R. Phinney to Mrs Etzwiler at the Sauk County Historical Society 11 August, 1989. George Olds Cooper to Mary Cooper, 24 May 1968 (in possession of Eleanor Wright).
370 Orr, 'Louis W.Claude: Madison Architect of the Prairie School'.
371 Letter from Sarah Harriet Withington to her sisters in Manchester, 12 May 1859 (in possession of Eleanor Wright). Sarah Withington, née Cooper was a cousin of Jane's old friend Jane Cooper (Raven).
372 Cannan, M., *Grey Ghosts and Voices*, p. 27.
373 Cannan, R., 'In Memoriam: Mary Louisa Cannan, an old Gallovidian'.
374 Cannan, M., *Grey Ghosts and Voices*, p. 27.
375 Legg, *Alfred Webb, the autobiography of a Quaker nationalist*, pp. 7-9.
376 *South Australia Register*, 13 February 1864; *South Australia Advertiser*, 13 February 1864.
377 http://www.llanelli-history.
378 Clough. B. A., *Anne J. Clough – Memoir*.
379 R.Adolphe Claude to JDC, 29 June 1858, DD262/addB5.
380 Cannan, Joanna, *Pray do not Venture*, pp.275-281.

Bibliography

Unpublished Sources

Cannan Family Papers: Trinity College, Oxford. DD262.

Cannan, David and Jane: Manuscripts Collection, National Library of Australia, MS401.

Catalogue of the Great Exhibition of the Works of Industry of all Nations, Spicer Bros, 1851. National Art Library, Victoria & Albert Museum, London.

Claude, Louis J: journal and papers in the Sauk County Historical Society, Wisconsin.

Clough, A, *Notebook 10*, 1847, Newnham College Cambridge.

Coleridge, Hartley, correspondence: Harry Ransom Humanities Research Centre, University of Texas at Austin.

Pollock, Andrew: *Observations of an Early Colonist during the years 1850-1852*, edited by Eleanor Wells, 1995, National Library of Australia, ref 642508.

Pollock, Andrew, correspondence and notebook, property of Eleanor Wells.

Webb, Alfred, *Autobiography*, Friends' Historical Library, Dublin.

Published sources

Ackroyd, Peter, *Dickens,* Guild Publishing, London, 1990.

Ackroyd, Peter, *London – the biography,* Vintage, London, 2001.

Annear, Robyn, *Bearbrass – Imagining Early Melbourne*, Black Inc/ Schwarz Publishing Pty Ltd, Melbourne, 2005.

Armstrong, Patrick, *The English Parson-Naturalist – a companionship between science and religion*, Gracewing, Leominster, 2000.

Ashton, Rosemary, *142 Strand,* Vintage, London, 2008.

Ashton, Rosemary, *Thomas and Jane Carlyle – Portrait of a Marriage*, Chatto & Windus, London, 2001.

Aughton, Peter, *Liverpool – A People's History,* Carnegie Publishing, Lancaster, 2008 edn.

Barringer, T., 'The Last of England', in P. Macdonald (ed), *Exiles and Emigrants – epic journeys to Australia in the Victorian Era*, National Gallery of Victoria, Melbourne, 2006.

Bertram, J. (ed), *The New Zealand Letters of Tom Arnold*, Aukland University Press, 1966.

Briggs, Asa, *Iron Bridge to Crystal Palace,* Thames and Hudson, London, 1977

Briggs, Asa, *Victorian Cities*, Odhams Press, London, 1963.

Briggs, Asa, *Victorian People*, Odhams/Pelican, Harmondsworth, 1954.

Camara, Benedita, 'The Image and Tourism Industry of Madeira 1850-1914', University of Madeira, 2003.

Cannan, Edwin, 'Pages from an Autobiography' in *The Clare Market Review*, XVI, 1935, pp. 16–17.

Cannan, Joanna, *Pray do not Venture,* Victor Gollancz, London, 1937.

Cannan, May Wedderburn, *Grey Ghosts and Voices,* Roundwood Press, Warwick, 1976.

Cannan, Rita, 'In Memoriam – Mary Louisa Cannan, an old Gallovidian', *The Gallovidian*, Summer 1912.

Casteras, S., 'Women and children last' in P. MacDonald (ed), *Exiles and Emigrants – epic journeys to Australia in the Victorian Era*, National Gallery of Victoria, Melbourne, 2006.

Charles Dickens, *David Copperfield*, originally published in 1849-50. Collins edition.

Claude, Mary, *Natural History in Stories* (1854); in the USA *Twilight Thoughts, Stories for Children and Child-Lovers*, Ginn and Co, Boston (with preface by Matthew Arnold), 1887.

Clough, B.A., *A Memoir of Anne Jemima Clough*, Edward Arnold, London, 1897.

Collini, S., 'Matthew Arnold' in *Oxford Dictionary of National Biography on-line 2004-9.*

Collier, S. and Slater, W., *A History of Chile*, Cambridge University Press, Cambridge, 1996.

Dubos, René and Jean, *The White Plague – tuberculosis, man and society*, Victor Gollancz, London, 1953.

Dyster, F.D., 'Madeira as a Residence for Invalids' in *Association Medical Journal,* 1(43),1853.

Evans, Ian, *The Australian Home*, Flannel Flower Press, Sydney, 1983.

Evans, Tony and Lycett Green, Candida, *English Cottages*, George Weidenfeld & Nicolson, London, 1982.

Farr, Diana, *Gilbert Cannan – a Georgian Prodigy*, Chatto & Windus, London, 1978.

Finer, S.E., *The Life and Times of Sir Edwin Chadwick*, Methuen, London, 1952.

Flanders, Judith, *The Victorian House – domestic life from childbirth to deathbed,* Harper Perennial, London, 2004.

Gaskell, Elizabeth, *North and South*, (originally published 1854-5), Penguin, Harmondsworth, 1970.

Gee,Lisa, (ed), *Bricks without Mortar: the selected poems of Hartley Coleridge*, Picador, London, 2005.

Greenhill, B. and Giffard, A., *Travelling by Sea in the Nineteenth Century – interior design in Victorian passenger ships.* Adam & Charles Black, London, 1972.

Gregory, T.E., 'Edwin Cannan: a personal impression' in *Economica*, November 1935, pp. 365-379.

Griggs, G.E. and E.L., *Letters of Hartley Coleridge*, Oxford University Press, Oxford, 1936.

Gwynne, Robin, *Huguenot Heritage*, Sussex Academic Press, Brighton, 2001.

Hammerton, James, *Emigrant Gentlewomen, genteel poverty and female emigration 1830-1914*, Croom Helm, London, 1979.

Hassam, Andrew, *Sailing to Australia – shipboard diaries by nineteenth century British emigrants*, Manchester University Press, Manchester, 1994.

Heasman, K., *Evangelicals in Action – an appraisal of social work in the Victorian Era*, Geoffrey Bles, London, 1962.

Herbert, Gilbert, *Pioneers of Prefabrication – the British contribution in the Nineteenth Century*. Johns Hopkins Press, Baltimore and London, 1978.

Honan, Park, *Matthew Arnold, A Life*, Weidenfeld and Nicolson, London, 1981.

Howe, A., *The Cotton Masters 1830-1860*, Clarendon Press, Oxford, 1984.

Hughes, Kathryn, *The Short Life and Long Times of Mrs Beeton*, Harper Perennial, London, 2006.

Jordan, Caroline, *Picturesque Pursuits – colonial women artists & the amateur tradition*, Melbourne University Press, Melbourne, 2005.

Johnston, Edwin, 'The Tin Tradition', *RIBA Journal* May 1981, pp. 35-40.

Kaplan, Fred, 'Thomas Carlyle' in *Dictionary of National Biography*, Oxford University Press, 2004.

Keneally, Tom, *The Commonwealth of Thieves – the story of the founding of Australia*, Chatto & Windus, London, 2006.

Kenny, Anthony, *Arthur Hugh Clough, A Poet's Life*, Continuum, London, 2005.

Kerr, Joan, *Dictionary of Australian Artists: painters, sketchers, photographers and engravers to 1870*. Oxford University Press, Melbourne, 1992. Entry for Jane Cannan.

Lee, C.H., *A Cotton Enterprise 1795-1840: a history of M'Connel & Kennedy, fine cotton spinners*, Manchester University Press, Manchester, 1972.

Legg, Marie-Louise, *Alfred Webb – the autobiography of a Quaker Nationalist*, Cork University Press, 1999.

Lewis, Miles, 'Notes on Jane Cannan's drawings' in *Victorian Historical Journal*, 81(1) 2010, pp.63-73.

Lewis, Miles, 'The Epigraphy of the Iron Tile' in *Construction History Society Newsletter* no 81, 2008.

Logan, D.A., *The Collected Letters of Harriet Martineau*, vol 3, Pickering & Chatto, London, 2007.

Lyall, Sutherland, *Dream Cottages – from Cottage Ornée to Stockbroker Tudor*, Robert Hale, London, 1988.

Macdonald, Patricia (ed), *Exiles and emigrants – epic journeys to Australia in the Victorian Era*, National Gallery of Victoria, Melbourne, 2006.

Marriner, S., *Rathbones of Liverpool*, 1845-73, Liverpool University Press, Liverpool, 1961.

Maw, Martin, 'Charles Cannan' in *Oxford Dictionary of National Biography*, 2004.

Mendez Beltrán, Luz Maria, *La Exportacion Minera en Chile 1800-1840*. Editorial Universitaria, Santiago, 2004.

Meyer, K. and P., *In the Shadow of the Himalayas – a photographic record by John Claude White 1883-1908*, Mapin Publishing, Ahmedabad, 2005.

Moore, M., 'Two views from Mr Pollock's window' in *Victorian Historical Journal*, June, 2012.

Moss, Stephen, *A Bird in the Bush – a social history of birdwatching*, Aurum, London, 2005.

Orr, G.W., 'Louis W. Claude: Madison Architect of the Prairie School' in *The Prairie School Review*, vol XIV. No Date.

Pattinson, G., *The Great Age of Steam on Windermere,* Windermere Nautical Trust, 1981.

Pieper, Shane 'Portable Iron Houses' in *This Australia*, Autumn 1983, pp. 28-31.

Peterson, Linda (ed), *Autobiography – Harriet Martineau*, Broadview Press, Toronto, 2007.

Reeder, Stephanie Owen, *The Vision Splendid*, National Library of Australia, Canberra ACT, 2011.

Serle, Geoffrey, *The Golden Age, A History of the Colony of Victoria 1851-1861*, Melbourne University Press, Melbourne, 1963.

Simey, M.B., *Charitable Effort in Liverpool in the Nineteenth Century*, Liverpool University Press, Liverpool, 1951.

Smith, F.B., *The Retreat of TB: 1850-1950*, Croom Helm, London, 1988.

Sutherland, Gillian, *Faith, Duty and the Power of Mind – the Cloughs and their circle 1820-1860*. Cambridge University Press, Cambridge, 2006.

Terry, M., 'The Voyage' in Macdonald, P (ed), *Exiles and Emigrants – epic journeys in the Victorian era,* National Gallery of Victoria, Melbourne, 2006.

Terry, Martin, *Cooee – Australia in the 19th Century*, National Library of Australia, Canberra, 2007.

Thompson, F.M.L., *The Rise of Respectable Society a social history of Victorian Britain 1830-1900,* Fontana, London, 1988.

Thomson, N., *Corrugated Iron Buildings*, Shire, Oxford, 2011.

Thomson, N. and Banfill, P., 'Corrugated-Iron Buildings: an endangered resource within the built heritage' in *Journal of Architectural Conservation*, No 1, 2005.

Todd, Barbara, *Harriet Martineau at Ambleside*, (containing Harriet Martineau's *A Year at Ambleside*) Bookcase, Carlisle, 2002.

Williams, D.M., 'Liverpool Merchants and the Cotton Trade 1820-1850' in Harris, J.R. (ed), *Liverpool and Merseyside – essays in the economic and social history of the port and its hinterland*, Frank Cass, London, 1969.

Woolcock, H., *Rites of Passage – emigration to Australia in the nineteenth century*. Tavistock, London, 1986.

Index

women: artists 7; obligations and
opportunities 2, 29-30, 35, 94,
96-97, 113-114, *see also* education,
spinsters, governesses
wool trade 38, 53, 91